SOLVED!

The "Mysterious" Disappearance of Jim Thompson,
the Legendary Thai Silk King

SOLVED!

The "Mysterious" Disappearance of Jim Thompson,
the Legendary Thai Silk King

Edward Roy De Souza

WORD ASSOCIATION PUBLISHERS
www.wordassociation.com
1.800.827.7903

Illustrations provided by Pak Ah Bee.

Photo credits: All Souls' Church (See Kok Shan, Curator, The Time Tunnel), Jim Thompson, the Thai Silk King (R. Rocklen), Lutheran Mission home (S. Murali), Moonlight bungalow (See Kok Shan, Curator, The Time Tunnel), Sunlight villa (Dollah bin Abdullah), Gunung Brinchang radio & television station (See Kok Shan, Curator, The Time Tunnel), Tanah Rata in the 1960s (See Kok Shan, Curator, The Time Tunnel), Jim Thompson circa 1961 (R. Rocklen).

Cover Design by Mark Ryan Eugenio.

ISBN: 978-1-59571-505-0
Library of Congress Control Number: 2009944204

Designed and published by

Word Association Publishers
205 Fifth Avenue
Tarentum, Pennsylvania 15084

www.wordassociation.com
1.800.827.7903

Dedicated to

Andrew Trevatt
Panadura Chandra Sena
Foong Chow Weng
Dr. Desmond Oon Seng Wah

Acknowledgements

I would like to thank the following for being a tremendous source of encouragement to me: Amin Bin Suratin, Andrew T.H. Lim, Ang Boon Tien, Ang Chua Whoo, Anthony A.S. Lewis, Anthony N. Allarey, Aloysius Hoeden, Ariffin Yassin, Barry White, Belly Anak Wah, Bernard Teo Tiat How, Brant LeBlanc, C.T. Lim, Callistus Leon D' Cruz, Ceril Jeris, Chang Kee Tong, Christopher K.Y. Liew, Clement Ng, Danny Teo, David Wong Kim, David Soh Jin Hoe, Dollah bin Abdullah, Dublin Anak Ijali, Eddie Lee Choon Guan, Estie Lim, Goh Lip Siah, Freddy Blight, Goh Khay Loon, Goh Tang Meng, Gordon Parnaby, Hermann Tay, Herold Thng, Htayy Win, Ibrahim Bin Mat, Irene Toh Lay Kuan, Ishak Mohamed Ali, James Koh, James Youngblood, Jayant Kumar Dey, Jeffrey Edwards, Jimmy Anak Ramba, Johnny Liso, Johnny Ong Koon Tin, Joseph Carp, Joseph Duggar, K. Sashidaran, Kenneth Chan Pong Heng, Kenneth Miller, Keramjit Singh, Kevin Banks, Koh Yeow Chiang, Komati Hari Prasad, Lee Kermit Kelling, Leong Weng Fatt, Lew Sai Keong, Lim Choon Teck, Lloyd Pereira, Lionel Chin, Lui Kean Hong, Malcolm Gallistan, Mark Ryan Eugenio, Michael Foster, Michael Hawkins, Michael Lee Ballard, Mohd. Azan bin Jaaffar, Mohamed bin Yim, Ng Boon Tong, Ng Chun Khin, Noorisham bin Abdullah, Pak Ah Bee, Philip Ong Meng Tiong, R. Rocklen, Rajendran Murigasin, Ray

Chan Weng Yong, Richard Teo Ah Fong, Robert Conceicao, Rodney Hui Ngee Chong, Roger Dennerly, Rony Hendarmin, Ronnie Lim, Rony Lee Nam San, S. Murali, S. Kathiravan, S. Sathiyannesan, Seah Kian Beng, Sebastian Lee, See Kok Shan, Seta Anak Padong, Sia Kwang Yiau, Sujoy Dey, Thomas Thiru, Toh Chin Siong, Toh Poh Soon, V. Soma (M.S. Velu), Ulrich Kuhlmann, Vincent Lee See Chai, Wong Koh Seng, Y.K. Choo, Yeo Ek Seng, Yeo Khim Hwa, Yong Per Muh and Zayani Suparman.

Contents

Prologue ix
Chapter One I
Chapter Two 3
Chapter Three 7
Chapter Four I3
Chapter Five I7
Chapter Six 2I
Chapter Seven 27
Chapter Eight 3I
Chapter Nine 37
Chapter Ten 39
Chapter Eleven 45
Chapter Twelve 55
Chapter Thirteen 57
Chapter Fourteen 73
Chapter Fifteen 77
Chapter Sixteen 8I
Chapter Seventeen 85
Chapter Eighteen 9I
Chapter Nineteen 95
Chapter Twenty 97
Chapter Twenty-One . . . . IOI
Chapter Twenty-Two I03
Postscript I09
Epilogue II3
Glossary I25

SOUTH
CHINA
SEA

PATTANI •

• PADANG BESAR
• SADAO

• SATUN

THAILAND

• KANGAR

ANDAMAN
SEA

□ ALOR STAR

KEDAH

• BETONG

• BUTTERWORTH

PENANG

KELANTAN

PERAK

MAP OF
NORTHWEST
MALAYSIA

• TAIPING

TANJONG
RAMBUTAN
TAMBUN •
IPOH □
SIMPANG PULAI •
GOPENG •

• BRINCHANG
• TANAH RATA
• RINGLET

PULAU
PANGKOR

• LUMUT

TAPAH •
BADOR •

PAHANG

■ KUALA
LUMPUR
SUBANG •

Prologue

The Cameron Highlands is renowned for its trails. Most of the paths are not well-kept. If you are planning a walk, do check with someone reliable as to whether the route you intend to take is indeed a suitable one.

Do not start a stroll late in the afternoon. Depending on its distance, some tracks can take as long as five hours to cover.

If, by chance, you lose your way, do not continue on from wherever you are. It would be wise to stop and return to where you first came from.

Whether you are going for a long walk or a short one, do not burden yourself with a whole load of items. A compass, a map, a whistle, a lighter, a water bottle, a torch, a knife and a raincoat are some of the things you should bring along with you.

Whatever it is, do not go for a hike all by yourself. If you intend to do so, do keep someone informed of your journey and the time you are expected to be back.

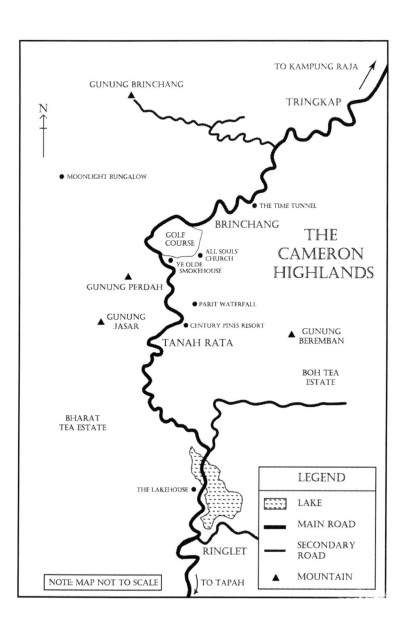

Chapter One

The hunt was for one man. He came to the Cameron Highlands for a short holiday. Two days later, he disappeared.

When he left the villa, no one was supposedly informed. His companions took it he had gone for an afternoon stroll. They expected him to be back by six. When he failed to do so, they began to sense something was amiss. To ascertain as to what was wrong, one of them got into his car and made his way to a nearby club. He had high hopes of meeting him along the way. But his drive in that direction drew a blank. For a while, he was in two minds as to what he should do next. Later, he went ahead and lodged a police report. He was told that word of his friend's disappearance would be made known to the settlements in the area. He was also informed if his friend failed to show up, an inquiry would be conducted the following morning.

On his return from the station, he came into contact with two visitors: one was his rental agent; the other was a major from the British army. After a short discussion, the guests left the estate and made their way to a nearby hill. The place was given a brief inspection but there was just no sign of him. Puzzled as to where he could be found, the pair revisited the cottage to see if they could gather more clues. At midnight, they left the house and made another attempt to find for him at a different location. But their second endeavor, like the first, produced no results.

At sunrise, about five policemen showed up at the bungalow. After taking down his particulars, they left the scene. Later that day, the police, with the help of thirty aborigines, carried out a search of their own. Their review was thorough but there was no trace of him. Before noon, word of his eclipse began to spread like wild fire. By now, more than a hundred people were looking high and low for him. The area was given a once-over but their effort proved fruitless.

The next day, a Tuesday, saw the biggest investigation mounted in Malaysian history. Tanah Rata, in fact, the whole of the Cameron Highlands, was agog with excitement. At ground level, troops crisscrossed the jungle. Above, a few helicopters were seen snooping over the treetops. In all, more than five hundred people were on the lookout for one man. It included no less than three hundred men from Perak's police field force, scores of tourists, residents, aborigines, American school students and British servicemen convalescing at the resort.

Overall, the probe was well organized. It was initially confined to within an eight-kilometer radius of 'Moonlight'. The areas covered were the Robinson waterfall, the golf course, the recreation ground, and the surrounding hills and ravines. Till late in the evening, no one was able to detect him. At the end of the day, the police came to two conclusions: Jim could either be trapped or he could have injured himself. But they were in no way discouraged. As far as they were concerned, he would somehow or other be able to find his way back.

Chapter Two

James (Jim) Harrison Wilson Thompson was born on March 21, 1906 in Greenville, Delaware, USA. He spent his early years of education at St Paul's boarding school. He later went on to enroll at Princeton. Postgraduate studies followed at the University of Pennsylvania's School of Architecture but he failed to get his degree at this institution due to his weakness in calculus.

In 1931, he settled for a career which involved the designing of homes for the East Coast rich. In the initial stages of his employment, he found his assignments to be rewarding. Later, the glamour of being an architect lost its allure for him. In 1941, he gave up his job and joined the Delaware National Guard Regiment. Just before the outbreak of the Second World War, he was transferred to a military outpost in Fort Monroe, Virginia. It was here that he got to know two persons, both of whom were to have a dramatic impact on his life.

The first was Patricia Thraves; the other, Edwin Black. Patricia was a voluptuous model. He was swept away by her beauty and magnetic mannerisms. After a whirlwind courtship, he went ahead and married her.

Edwin was a fresh graduate from the military college of West Point. He encouraged Jim to join a new outfit which was known as the Office of Strategic Services (OSS). Without any hesitation, Jim did so.

He discovered his new job at the OSS – the frontrunner of the Central Intelligence Agency – to be a lot more interesting. As a spy, he was given a free hand to put his raw talents and creativity to good use. But there was a drawback to his career: it was required of him to be away from home at short notice. However, this did not in the least bother him.

His first call of duty was with the French resistance forces in North Africa. Later, arrangements were made for him to be sent to Europe. At the height of the Second World War, large areas of the Continent were under the control of the Germans. Jim, who was now approaching forty, was assigned the task of destroying their communication centers. It was not an easy task but he managed to perform his duties to expectation. Within a span of six months, he was promoted twice – first to the rank of captain, then to the position of major.

While he was engaged in Europe, his wife began to turn her back on him. He came to realize there was now a growing coldness between the two of them. To get his mind off her, he requested for a posting in East Asia. Eight weeks later his application was accepted.

His initial posting was in the volatile China-Burma-India war zone. While based there, he was promoted to the rank of lieutenant colonel. His next station was in Ceylon where he was put in charge of the pro-Allied *Seri Thai* or Free Thai Movement. The guerrillas under him were trained to carry out clandestine activities against their occupiers. For months they were taught how to live off the land. Their training was rigorous and it received the support of Pridi Panomyong and Seni Pramoj. Pridi, a brilliant French-trained lawyer, was at that time serving as regent to King Ananda Mahidol. Seni, on the other hand, was a Thai politician who was based in the United States. Both Pridi and Seni were of one mind – they were determined to see the Japanese out of their country. In 1945, arrangements were made to help liberate the country. But two developments held back the plans of the Free Thai Movement: on August 6, the atomic bomb fell on Hiroshima; three days later, Nagasaki was hit. For the next few days, Jim and his group were instructed to stay put at wherever they were operating. Six days later, they left their base and got themselves ready to penetrate into central Thailand. Their role was to get the locals to go against the Japanese. Their plan, however, did not come to pass. While they were heading for Thailand, they were informed that the war in Asia had come to an end. The bombings of Hiroshima and Nagasaki proved to be a success – tens of thousands perished from the impact. Fearing further destruction to their other cities, the Japanese opted to surrender. This was followed by the withdrawal of their troops from the area. With their departure, peace was once again restored to the Asia-Pacific region.

Chapter Three

After the war, Jim flew in to Bangkok. He realized the city was a lot different from what he had made it out to be. On land, the people moved around in a pedicab or *samloh*. Off land, the traffic commuted via the town's canals or *klongs*. On the whole, he noticed the Thais were not only proud of their culture; by nature, they were charming as well.

"Thailand," he observed, "reminds me of the Delaware of my boyhood. When I was young, I always had the feeling the world around me was full of surprises. I consider Thailand to be one such place."

While he was in Thailand, he was assigned to the US embassy to serve as its military attaché.

One of his first friends was Constance (Connie) Mangskau. After her release from prison, she worked as an interpreter for the Allied Services based in Bangkok. "Jim," she said, "was enraptured by Bangkok. It was as if he had arrived somewhere he had long belonged to."

While he was still in service, he made up his mind to stay on in Thailand. As the Allied forces began withdrawing, he started to cast around for a career.

During his free time, he took the occasion to explore the remote areas of the country. His upland visits sometimes took him to the borders of Laos and Myanmar.

In 1946, it came to his knowledge that the Oriental hotel in Bangkok was up for sale. He partnered Germaine Krull, Prince Bhanu Yukol, General Chai Prateepasen, Pote Sarasin and John Webster to buy over the hotel. They each contributed US$250. The hotel – which was leased to the Japanese during the war – was in a bad shape when he and the others took over the running of the place. But he was in no way discouraged by its poor state and condition. He was positive it had the potential of being what it once used to be.

After spending a year in Thailand, it dawned on him he had to decide as to whether he wanted to go on being in the army or to seek a discharge from it. Of the two, he chose the latter. That same year, he left Thailand for America. While he was in his hometown, he met up with his wife and tried to bring their nine-month-old marriage into line. During the attempted reconciliation, he persuaded her to settle down with him in Thailand. Suffice it to say, she was not in favor of it. Their parting of ways had a great effect on him. He came back to Thailand a broken man. For the next few months, he was positive his hotel venture would take off. It never did. While working on its improvement, he had some differences with his associates and this resulted in him giving up his shares altogether.

While looking around for a profession, he found himself spending more time exploring the outskirts of the country. On some of his visits, he spotted the presence of looms in a number of homes. On inquiring about their significance, he was told they were for the weaving of silk. When handed a piece of the hand-finished cloth, he realized it was unlike any other he had laid his hands on. From what he knew, he had struck a treasure. His father had been in the textile business for years. While assisting him, he developed a fine eye for judging various types of materials – one of them was silk. In all his travels, he never came across anything more exquisite than Thai silk. But what surprised him was this:

in spite of its richness, Thai silk was relatively unknown to the outside world; it was not even sold on a large scale in Thailand. Each family wove just enough for their own use. After giving it serious thought, he was convinced it had commercial possibilities. But there were three production aspects which had to undergo a change: firstly, the fabric had to be woven into saleable lengths; secondly, the dyes had to be replaced with aniline; lastly, a fresh set of designs had to be incorporated into the product to help create an interest in the material.

Initially, he had a hard time putting his ideas across. His inability to communicate with the weavers was one drawback; their resistance to change was another. But he remained tenacious, going on to search the country's weavers. Finally he came into contact with a community of weavers from Baan Krua in Bangkok's Ratchatewi district. After some persuasion, they were prepared to give his ideas a try.

In 1947, he bought about US$100 worth of their merchandise and made his way to New York. While he was there, he got to know Edna Woolman Chase, then the editor of *Vogue*. She was impressed with the silk he had brought along with him. Later, without his even knowing it, she engaged Valentina Schlee, a New York designer, to fashion a dress out of his material. A few weeks later, the outfit was featured in her monthly publication. This marked the revival of Thai silk which had all but vanished due to cheaper imports from Europe and Japan.

Jim was particularly excited that silk was becoming a hit among the fashion-conscious. A year later, he returned to Thailand. While moving around, he chanced upon a shop which sold Thai silk. That same year, an opportunity came his way. He met George Barrie, an old-time friend from Santa Monica, California. He brought George to the Chinese shop. George was amazed at what he saw. At first sight, he knew Thai silk had the potential of being a marketable item. Towards the end of 1948, George partnered Jim to form the Thai Silk Company. It was capitalized at US$25,000. They each bought eighteen per cent of its shares. The remaining sixty-four per cent were sold to both Thai and foreign investors.

The real breakthrough came in 1951 when designer Irene Sharaff made use of Thai silk fabrics for the Rogers and Hammerstein musical, *The King and I.* From then on, the company prospered. Three years after its founding, the shareholders of the company enjoyed a one hundred per cent dividend. Their staff too was rewarded with three months' wages plus twenty per cent of the company's profits.

Jim's discovery of the industry raised many an eyebrow. Despite being a newcomer, the company managed to outgrow its beginnings. By the mid-1960s, it had to compete with more than a hundred establishments selling Thai silk.

On the whole, there was no big secret to the company's style of doing business; in essence, it operated much like a cooperative. Several weaving groups worked for the organization. People who owned from four to a hundred looms produced the silk. The firm provided them with dyes, designs and financial support. On their part, they had to adhere to the requirements of the company.

Jim used to visit the different looms every morning. During his daily rounds he made it a point to check on the previous day's work. His formula for success was not as complex as what one would make it out to be. It hinged on two factors.

"In the first instance," he said, "we run a dependable operation. Whenever we come up with a pattern or color that sells well, we make sure we stick to its exact formula. That way, our customers can rest assured that when they re-order, they will get a consistent product."

"Equally important," he mentioned, "is that the cottage industry in this part of the world is more significant than what most people realize. Most of the weavers in this area either don't care or don't need to know who are buying their products. But it is necessary for us to know what our customers' tastes and requirements are."

Jim added, "The Thai silk-weavers technique is hundreds of years old. Every child learns how to weave but each family weaves only enough for its own needs. Their styles and colors are not suitable for foreign consumption. It took us a lot of time to know what the world markets required. It makes no difference to us as to how well we know our clients. What really matters is whether they like our products or not.

"(Whatever it is), I always try to keep everything as Thai as possible. Quite a considerable amount of my time is spent at the National Museum doing research on designs."

He expounded, "I must say silk in itself portrays a great deal of glamour. It has an aura of exotic mystery and richness about it. For centuries, it has been the fabric of kings and queens. From the way our sales are moving, I can safely say our customers are beginning to dress like royalty."

Nobility aside, Jim also believed in man's right to work, his right to earn a profit and his right to choose the kind of work he favored. To a large extent, nearly everyone who was engaged in the industry benefited from this philosophy.

Jim's first dealing with a weaver was in 1948. Nineteen years later, that same man was still working for him. Instead of using one loom, the weaver had more than a hundred. For his contribution, the company paid him and his workers well over US$20,000 per month. But he was not an exceptional case. The seventy-one other families who had contracts with the company also earned equally good incomes. In return, they provided work for no less than three thousand other weavers.

Chapter Four

Jim was unlike any other figure in Southeast Asia. He was an American, an ex-architect, a retired army officer, a one-time spy, a silk merchant, a millionaire and a renowned collector of antiques. Most of his treasures, if not all, were amassed since the day he first came to Thailand. As time slipped by, his assortment outgrew its surroundings and this left him with not much of a choice but to find a place to house them. For some time, he did toy with the idea of constructing a home which was unlike any other in the region. Apart from serving as his place of residence, it also had to double up as a repository for his artifacts. It was a tall order, no doubt, but he managed to achieve it nevertheless. Using parts of old up-country houses – some as old as a hundred years – he succeeded in completing his 'House on the Klong' in 1959. It was basically a colony of six dwellings which were reassembled into his much larger place of abode. The units were dismantled and brought over via river from the ancient Thai capital of Ayutthaya. On arrival, they were offloaded and pieced together. Of the six, three were left untouched.

In his quest for authenticity, he saw to it that the structures were elevated a full floor above the ground. During the construction stage, he added his own touches to the buildings by positioning, for instance, a central staircase indoors rather than having it outside. Along the way, he also reversed the wall panels of his quarters so that it now faced inside instead of it having an external orientation.

While the outcome of his domicile may not have been somewhat traditional, it could be taken he did have a fondness for it. After he was through with its creation, he went about filling his premises with the items he had collected in the past. Scattered about his rooms were scores of Chinese blue-and-white Ming pieces, Belgian glass, Cambodian stone figures, Victorian chandeliers, five-colored Bencharong, Thai stone images, Burmese statues and a dining table which was once used by King Rama V of Thailand.

In all, his 'House on the Klong' took up close to a hectare in area. The garden around the habitation was nothing short of a mini-jungle. On it stood a typical Thai spirit altar.

It took Jim almost a year to put his house in order. On completion, it turned out to be a masterpiece. The press were quick to describe it as "one of the wonders of the East." In several ways, they were right: till today, it stands out as one of Bangkok's most charming attractions. His mansion, which is open to the public, is presently situated near Klong Maha Nog at the end of Soi Kasemsong II, which is, incidentally, just across from the National Stadium on Rama I Road.

Practically every night there was a dinner guest at his villa. Hollywood stars, entrepreneurs, novelists and politicians – they all came visiting at his museum-like home. Some of the many who came by to see him included personalities such as Henry Ford II, William Fulbright, Cecil Beaton, Doris Duke, Truman Capote, Lyndon Johnson, Ethel Merman, Adlai Stevenson, Tennessee Williams, Katherine Hepburn, Barbara Hutton, Robert Kennedy, Ann Baxter and even Prince Michael of Greece. Somerset Maugham once wrote to him after having dinner at his place: "Jim, you not only have beautiful things but what is rare, you have displayed them beautifully."

Contrary to popular belief, Jim's circle of friends did not center merely on the rich and famous. It included, among others, those who had no social standing or tourists who used to stop at his shop. Whoever or whatever they were, he was always on hand to see to it they were merrily entertained. Outwardly, many a guest found him to be a warm and compassionate person. Inwardly, very few were aware of his deep loneliness and his desire to be loved. On the whole, he was an approachable person. It was not only a joy conversing with him; equally interesting, he was also a good listener. However, he did have a weakness, a weakness which no one dared to talk about, namely, his fuming temper. If he felt he was being belittled, he would respond by telling off the offender. If he was made out to be dishonest, he would retaliate by not talking to that person.

In spite of his wealth, Jim was, in many ways, a simple man. His dressing was in no way outlandish. As for food, he was no gourmet. It could be said he was a caring person. Many who knew him well benefited from his kind-heartedness. The local School for the Blind was one example. On the quiet, he saw to it that enough funds were sent its way.

While his silk business continued to grow, so too did his popularity. The press was continually at his heels. He could have ignored them had he wanted to but he never did. Over time, his reputation grew to legendary proportions and, with this, he came to be known by many names. Of the many, two stood out among the rest: the foreign media was fond of addressing him as 'The Thai Silk King'; the Thai press, on the other hand, coined the phrase 'The Thai Silk Millionaire'. There is no doubt he did have a million dollars but, it was not from his business; it was actually from an inheritance. Prior to his ceasing to be seen, his annual income was close to US$33,000. For quite some time, he did own a total of eighteen per cent of his company's shares. To a certain extent, the dividends derived from his shares did help to augment his income but this did not last for long. As the years went by, his share in the company began to shrink. This had nothing to do with poor management; it had a lot to do with his exchanging them for the favors which came his way.

Chapter Five

There is no doubt Jim was, in very many ways, responsible for bringing the Thai silk industry to the forefront. It started off with nothing new; over time, Thai silk, which was unknown to the outside world, grew in both demand and popularity. Jim was especially proud of his contribution; it gave him a sense of joy and accomplishment. However, his success came with a price. To a large extent, it drained him.

His friends were aware his work was slowly beginning to have an effect on his health. Out of good cheer, they encouraged him to take a break. He did so.

On Friday, March 24, 1967, he, together with Mrs. Constance Mangskau, 59, took the occasion to holiday at Malaysia's Cameron Highlands. Located on the northwestern tip of Pahang, the tourist center is one of Malaysia's most extensive hill stations. It is about fifty kilometers off the main Kuala Lumpur-Ipoh-Butterworth road at Tapah, Perak. Strange as it may seem, the hamlet is not at all easy to pinpoint on any map. This is due to the fact that the dwellings tend to occupy whatever land area that is readily available along the main road.

Since its coming into being, the refuge has long been a favorite stopover for the many who want to escape from the heat of the lowlands. It got its name from William Cameron, a British surveyor who was commissioned by the then colonial government to map out the area in 1885. In a statement concerning his mapping expedition, William mentioned he saw "a vortex in the mountains, while for a (reasonably) wide area we have gentle slopes and plateau land."

When approached, the late Sir Hugh Low, the Resident of Perak, expressed the wish of developing the flat terrain as a "sanatorium, health resort and open farmland." A narrow path to "Cameron's Land" was then carved through the dense jungle. Nothing much happened after that. Forty year later, Sir George Maxwell visited the territory and decided to transform the place into a settlement. A development committee was formed in 1925. Once the road was constructed, the British and the locals moved in to settle on the slopes of the mountain. They were soon followed by tea planters and vegetable growers who found the fertile soil, good drainage and cool climate to be especially suitable for the growing of their crops.

The haven, which is nestled at an altitude of about 1,600 to 2,200 meters, is basically made up of three distinct villages, namely, Ringlet, Tanah Rata and Brinchang. All three are separated from one another by a considerable distance.

Ringlet, which is about fifty kilometers from the turn-off at Tapah, is the first stop of the region. It does boast of a number of places to stay in but most fun-seekers prefer to move north where there is more to enjoy. But the journey up is not as easy as one would make it out to be. The road is not only narrow; it is also just as winding as well. Negotiating its endless array of hairpin bends is indeed a skill in itself.

About fourteen kilometers away is the other Highland town of Tanah Rata. It has a population of more than 12,000, most of who are engaged in the hospitality business. Apart from sweet-smelling dahlias, roses, tulips and chrysanthemums, the district is also noted for being the prime center for a wide range of social and recreational activities.

Further on is Brinchang where rows of vegetable farms form part of the landscape. It is approximately five kilometers from Tanah Rata and is one of the highest points in Malaysia which is accessible by car. Like Tanah Rata, Brinchang has an extensive assortment of hotels from which to choose. Close to the top of its peak is a radio and television station. During fair weather, one can easily get a view of the Straits of Melaka which is located to the west of the retreat.

On the whole, the Camerons can be regarded as a world in miniature. It occupies the smallest constituency in the state of Pahang. To the north, its boundary touches that of Kelantan; to the west, it shares part of its border with Perak. During the day, the temperature seldom soars above 25°C. At night, it is the opposite: the temperature can sometimes drop to as low as 6°C. The cool climate makes it an ideal place for tea to be grown. The growing of tea had its beginnings in 1926 when the British started the first plantations with saplings brought over from India. Today, there are no less than five tea estates at the center.

Apart from tea, the sanctuary is also noted for its insect life, trails, waterfalls, soaring peaks, scenic spots and last but not least, its awe-inspiring natives. The natives or aborigines are basically jungle dwellers. Approximately 100,000 people in peninsula Malaysia come under the general classification of 'Orang Asli'. It is actually an all-encompassing term used to describe the different ethnic groups such as the Batek, Chewong, Jah Hut, Jakun, Jehai, Jengjeng, Kensiu, Kentaq Bong, Lanoh, Mabetisek, Medrique, Mintil, Mos, Orang Kanaq, Orang Selitar, Sabum, Semaq Beri, Semnam, Semai, Semelai, Temiar, Temoq, Temuan and Tonga. Their social system is unique in the sense that it hinges on the concept of avoiding conflict as far as possible. Decisions within the tribe are usually made during collective discussions and the role of the chief is strictly that of a mediator.

The traditional weapon which an aborigine is allowed to own is that of a blowpipe. It is actually a tube-like structure which is made from bamboo. The length of the pipe varies according to one's taste or fancy. By force of the breath, poison darts are discharged from it.

The aborigines of the enclave are believed to have migrated into the area long before the arrival of the Malays. On the surface, their lifestyle has always been made out to be backward. But this has gradually changed over the years. While many have left to take up residence in the nearby towns, there are still some who prefer to treat the wilderness as their home. The woodlands they live in can be considered as inhospitable but the challenges it has to offer are indeed varied. Many who have been to the Highlands have acknowledged this to be so. Jim was no exception. He found the appeal of the forest to be irresistible. So too did his friend, Dr. Ling Tien Gi, a Singaporean-Chinese chemist and Helen, his white American-born wife.

Chapter Six

The Lings were the owners of Moonlight bungalow, a Tudor-style dwelling which is located at A47, Jalan Kamunting, 39000, Tanah Rata. Situated about two kilometers from Jalan Besar, the address is somewhere between the districts of Tanah Rata and Brinchang.

As far as Jim and Constance were concerned, this was their third visit to the Ling's estate. It could be said the foursome not only got along well; equally interesting, all four shared the same love for the jungle.

When they met on Friday, their get-together did not take up much of their time. This was due to the fact they reached the villa at different times: the first to do so was Dr. Ling; Jim and Constance were next; Helen, who was tied up with a business deal, arrived at eight. The trip up was no joke – they found it to be long and taxing. After dinner, they retired to their respective rooms for a rest.

The next morning, while the two ladies were engrossed with their conversation, Jim and Dr. Ling took the opportunity to explore the tropical rainforest for themselves. They were equally anxious to try out a new trail which Dr. Ling had previously discovered. After the hike, they were supposed to meet up with the two ladies at a nearby club. But their plan almost turned into a nightmare: while they were in the wilderness, it became obvious they were lost. When they failed to show up, the women became upset. For a moment, Helen did entertain the thought of wanting to call the police. It was only after eleven that Jim spotted a narrow stream. "Don't worry," he told Dr. Ling. "Follow me along this stream and we'll get out." They traced it and in a matter of an hour, they were back to familiar surroundings. Both of them were worn out when they strolled into the club. During the hike, Dr. Ling had pulled a ligament and it was clear he was a bit shaken by his morning adventure. But not so for Jim. He was elated the two of them got lost along the way. While he was at the clubhouse, he gave Constance and Helen a briefing of what transpired while he and Dr. Ling were in the woods.

When his narration was over, the party left the place and returned to their home. After lunch, they agreed to have an afternoon siesta. The Lings shared a large bedroom at the front of the building. As for Constance, she occupied a much smaller room which was next to theirs. In the case of Jim, he retired to the remaining room which was near the staircase.

At about 4.30pm they got up for some tea. Later, they headed for Ye Olde Smokehouse to have dinner with Dr. Einar Ammundsen. Dr. Ammundsen, Jim's physician, was at the hill station by coincidence. After dinner, they decided to call it a day.

The subsequent morning, they got up early to attend a religious service at a nearby chapel. It was reported, their program for the day was to spend some time in church followed by a picnic at Gunung (Mount) Brinchang. While the rest were getting themselves ready, Jim informed them he would be taking a walk to the main road. Along the way, he met up with them and they all drove on to Tanah Rata to attend the Easter services at All Souls' Church.

When the services came to an end, they supposedly headed for Moonlight to collect a hamper which they had put aside for their picnic.

While they were at their quarters, Jim surprised them by suggesting that the picnic be held in the garden instead. For a moment, the others were confused by his sudden change of mind. After some persuasion, they managed to win him over to their original plan.

The supposed drive to the mountain took more than an hour. At the picnic, it was reported Jim was not his usual self; he seemed bothered by something that was either said or done. For a short interval, none of them was able to make out what was on his mind. Sensing a funny change in his character, the Lings suggested he take a rest. He declined their offer and preferred instead that their outing be called off. Not wanting to be a source of disappointment to him, the trio complied with his request.

They claimed they left the site at around 1.20pm and got back to Moonlight at about 2.30pm. Since they had no other plans for the afternoon, it was published that Jim chose to sit in the hall while the rest opted for their rooms.

Later, he got up and left the house. After he had gone, it became apparent he left behind his suit jacket, a pill box, a packet of cigarettes and a lighter.

Dr. Ling remembered hearing the sound of footsteps "pass by my bedroom door about 3.30pm." He presumed it was Jim going out for a stroll. As such, he did not take the trouble to ascertain if this was really the case.

When Jim left the complex, it was alleged that no one was kept informed. During his last visit to the outpost, it was disclosed he was stung by hornets about a kilometer from Moonlight. He did inform Constance and his other friends he would like to visit this spot on his next trip. Whether he did so, no one really knows. But one thing is for sure: he did leave Moonlight for an afternoon stroll; he failed to return by 6pm.

After six, Dr. Ling got into his car and took a slow drive to a nearby club. He was confident he would meet Jim along the way. He never did. When he came home, he was puzzled as to where Jim could have gone to. Later, Constance gave a call to Dr. Ammundsen to find out if Jim had visited him at Ye Olde Smokehouse. Dr. Ammundsen told her that Jim did not.

By now the Lings and Constance began to sense something was amiss. Out of concern for his friend, Dr. Ling called his rental agent to inform him about of Jim's absence. He felt since he knew the area rather well, word of Jim's whereabouts would soon be forthcoming. This, however, did not come to pass. At 8.30pm, he went ahead and lodged a police report.

The police were surprised the man they had to deal with was no stranger. After filing his report, Dr. Ling was assured that word of his missing friend would be filtered down to the settlements in the area. He was also told if Jim failed to show up, an inquiry would be conducted the following morning.

On his return from the station, two visitors called at his residence: one was his rental agent; the other was a major from the British army. After a short discussion, the pair left the estate and made their way for a nearby hill. The place was briefly inspected but they drew a blank. Undaunted, the two revisited the cottage to see if they could gather more clues.

At midnight, they left the house and made another attempt to find for him at a different location. But their second endeavor, like the first, produced no results.

The Lings and Constance did not fall off to sleep that night. They stayed awake in the hope that Jim would show up when least expected.

At daybreak, about five policemen appeared at the chalet. After studying Jim's passport details, they left the scene. Just after they had gone, Constance phoned Barry Cross, her son-in-law, and informed him of Jim's predicament. After the call, Barry notified General Edwin Black and gave him the news.

Later that morning, the police, with the help of thirty aborigines, combed the area. The survey was intensive but there was just no trace of Jim. Before noon, news of his disappearance began to spread. By then, more than a hundred people were on the lookout for him, to no avail.

The following day (March 28), the biggest hunt in Malaysian history was staged. The police came prepared to handle the task on hand. Most of the teams came complete with walkie-talkies, loud hailers and field telephones. A select group was armed with pistols and sub-machine guns. In the late afternoon, two British Royal Army Air Corps helicopters en route to Seremban made a stop at the depot. They were asked to assist with the exploration. After getting the clearance from their superiors, they did so.

The sweep of the forest was fairly thorough. It went on without a break. Till late in the evening, no one was able to find Jim. The police concluded that Jim could either be trapped or accidentally injured. However, they were convinced he would somehow or other be able to make his way back. His previous jungle-survival training, they reasoned, would be sufficient to see him through whatever difficulties he was in.

Chapter Seven

On Wednesday, March 29, the police were provided with some pointers which they found to be helpful in their quest to locate Jim.

Che Fatimah binte Mohamed Yeh, 24, a cook at the Lutheran Mission bungalow, told Superintendent A.S. Nathan she saw Jim on Sunday at about 4pm.

"I was in the kitchen," she said, "when I saw him come up the road. He had on a white shirt and a pair of gray slacks. He stopped for a while to take a look at the garden. While looking at the plants, he did not speak to anyone. A short while later, he left the premises and headed the same way from where he came."

In a separate report, a servant at the Overseas Mission Fellowship mansion informed the police she saw a man who resembled Jim standing on a plateau opposite the property. According to her, he was there at around 4pm. After thirty minutes or so, he was not to be seen.

The last person who saw him was an employee of the Eastern Hotel (which is now known as the Century Pines Resort). He was sure he saw someone who looked like Jim heading in the direction of the track which led to the golf course.

The police considered all three clues to be useful. But the sighting of the second witness gave them the impression that Jim could have wandered over a nearby ridge. Beyond it is a forked path: one led to the dense, triple-canopy jungle; the other circled back. The police party, which was divided into several groups, did not cover this sector. At the start of the operation, they were of the opinion it was unlikely of Jim to have gone in that direction. To begin with, the area is vastly impenetrable. To explore it would only mean a waste of their time. But the testimony of the second witness made them think otherwise. After some deliberation, a fresh set of orders was issued for the area to be combed.

Later that afternoon, the members of the press who had gathered at Tanah Rata were told that plans were underway for a change in the leadership's command. They were informed that Assistant Commissioner of Police (ACP) Yusoff Khan, who was put in charge of the operation, would be recalled to Ipoh. Before his departure ACP Khan notified the press that the police were of the impression "if Jim had wandered beyond the ridge, it would take several more days before he would be found."

This estimation on his part left many a resident worried about Jim's fate. The area, they reasoned, could be freezing cold at night. By virtue of the fact he was not properly attired, most locals were prepared to conclude that Jim's odds of surviving were indeed slim.

Regardless of the situation he was in, the casting about for him went on without much of a break. At sunset, the police were told that a tiger was spotted in the vicinity of Brinchang. They were informed that two villagers saw the creature while it was in the process of dragging away their dog. On receiving the news, a sizable portion of the police field force was ordered to backtrack. Arrangements were later made for them to be re-deployed to the county's northwestern sector.

On the whole, the police regarded the disappearance of Jim to be somewhat puzzling. After dinner, they had a hard time trying to figure out what could have possibly happened to him. It was this uncertainty that left them in a situation where they had no choice but to hold on to several views. Of these, they did not rule out the possibility that he could have been kidnapped. Jim, they noted, had been to the Camerons on three or more occasions. While on vacation, he was in the habit of moving around alone. He was usually seen at the upland's lake and forested areas. The police were suspicious whether an organized gang could have kidnapped him while he was all by himself. But there was a twist to his vanishing which left them in want of an answer. From their experience, ransoms are usually demanded within a forty-eight hour time frame. Since the start of the operation, there had been no demand for any ransom.

Ransom or no ransom, the police went on with their investigations. By then, they had spent more than seventy-two hours looking for Jim. The scouting, which was conducted in shifts, went on round-the-clock. With the exit of ACP Khan, Superintendent A.S. Nathan was put in charge of the operation. The handing over of duties was smooth, there being no reported change in the mission's overall strategy.

Chapter Eight

The sudden disappearance of Jim came as a shock to many; this was especially so for those who knew him rather well. But they were not troubled by the news that came their way. One such person who felt that way was Constance. According to her, they had known each other for more than twenty years. When asked about his character, she remembered a trip which they made to the Himalayas a couple of years ago.

"During the trip," she said, "Jim went missing… for almost four weeks. We spent a lot of our time looking for him in the mountains. The other members of our team and I were surprised when he showed up at the end of our heartbreaking search. He was certainly weak and exhausted when he got back."

"Jim," she noted, "was in the habit of losing himself. He would turn up when least expected. I have a feeling he was in one of his unpredictable moods when he ventured on his latest jaunt into the jungle."

Dr. Ammundsen, Jim's long-time friend, took a similar view. He believed there was "still hope he might be wading downstream or downtrail. For all you know, he could show up at a settlement… a few kilometers to the east or elsewhere."

In Thailand, the news of his vanishing was somewhat different: it was nothing but a mixed bag of guesses and hope. Some were prepared to conclude he was as good as gone; others, however, were sure he would return on his own. Astrologers who were consulted were of the impression he was "still alive and in a matter of time he would be found."

In Malaysia, the outlook amongst some of his friends was a lot dimmer. As the days passed, they began to doubt as to whether he was still alive. "One can go on walking," they noted, "without meeting another human being in the tangled vegetation." Based on this reasoning, they were resigned to the possibility that he would not be discovered.

In Bangkok, the Thai Silk Company took the news of his eclipse more seriously. The officials of the company were positive something amiss could have happened to him. Charles U. Sheffield, 40, who was appointed acting manager, announced that "a generous reward (of US$10,000) will be paid by the Thai Silk Company to any person or persons" who succeeded in finding Jim. The offer was made on Wednesday, March 29, that is, three days after he went astray. This incentive was a close follow-up to the strong rumors in the Thai capital that he could have been kidnapped and taken to another country.

Apart from this, two other enticements were also declared. On her part, Constance affirmed she was more than willing to hand out a gift to anyone who knew where Jim could be located. She left the details of her "handsome reward" with the police at Tanah Rata. The Malaysian police, in line with tradition, also came up with a remuneration amounting to RM10,000 (about US$3,000). The payment, which was approved by the Inspector General of Police, was valid for a period of three months.

The day after the Thai Silk Company announced their reward, a young lady showed up at the company's premises. She informed the staff she knew something about Jim's predicament. Determined to give anything a try, the staff ushered her into a dimly lit room. A collection of candles and joss sticks were lit and placed under a white piece of cloth. While she was praying, the employees kept their focus on the fabric which was hung on the wall. They were confident the 'screen' would show them something about the situation Jim was in. To their great disappointment, they saw nothing. But their guest swore she saw something. When asked what it was, she avowed she saw Jim being held captive by two gunmen. All three were in the jungle.

Over at Tanah Rata, a *ton-kee* (medium) came up with a different interpretation. Thong Weng, 29, a part-time painter, proclaimed to two of his followers that Jim was "alive but possessed by evil spirits." Before announcing this to Shee Voon Chin, a sundry-shop proprietor and Raymond Chan, a food contractor, he went into a number of trances. His first was on Wednesday, March 29. After coming out of his spell, he predicted Jim would make his way back to Moonlight "on his own." He also said that this would take place "at about 9am the next day." But nothing of that sort came to pass. Not to be outdone, he spent the later part of the morning working himself into a double trance. He pleaded with the spirit world for a hint as to where Jim could be found. In all, it took him about an hour to come out of his incantation.

After regaining his normal senses, he informed Voon Chin and Raymond that "Jim is still being possessed by evil spirits." He went on to say that Jim could be detected "in a hole which is not far from Moonlight." He added, "During their survey, a few parties did pass by this spot without noticing him. He tried to call out to them but, being weak, his calls went unheard."

On hearing this, Voon Chin and Raymond gathered some of their employees to conduct a survey of their own. Armed with gongs and cymbals, they took the route which Thong Weng had instructed them to embark. Their scanning of the woods was thorough. They took vigilant note of the large trees along the way. Their bases were carefully checked for holes. Depressions that were covered in thick ground cover were not only checked but also double-checked. Overall, the group spent about two hours looking for Jim. By noon they gave up their pursuit and returned to the temple. They approached Thong Weng and asked him why they were unable to find Jim. When pressed for an answer, Thong Weng was quick to point out that they all went in the wrong direction. To satisfy their needs, he went into another trance. He later led the group for a brief inspection of the forest. The result of their exploration was nothing but a flop. He later told a police source he would be heading for Ipoh to consult a "higher medium." He promised to revert with an answer. He never did.

Whatever the mystic predicted, the police took no notice of it. Their attention was more focused on the likely areas where Jim could be detected. During their air mission on March 29, the pilot of a Royal Malaysian Air Force helicopter enquired of the aboriginal settlers as to whether they had seen the missing man. They informed him they did not. Before leaving, the pilot left word with them to keep the police informed if they encountered Jim. He also reminded them not to harm him.

While the pilot hop scotched from one settlement to another, on the ground were no less than a hundred officers and men who went about scouring the rainforest. Their senses were alert for any sign that may give them a clue to Jim's whereabouts. Led by Assistant Superintendent of Police (ASP) Sarain Singh, they reported back in the afternoon without any success.

When questioned by the press, ASP Singh had this to say: "There is no new development today. But we're still hopeful."

The police were hopeful but two groups lost hope along the way. The first were the volunteers from the British army; the other was the students from Dalat American School. Both parties called off their hunt after the lunch break.

Later in the afternoon there was a slight change in events: Dr. Ling left the district for Singapore; at Moonlight, Helen and Constance continued to wait for Jim's return. They wanted to take care of him in the event he showed up. Helen informed the media she took the view that, "despite the dim prospects, everything must be all right with him. We will remain here to see the end of this search. We will be here for as long as we know and believe he will come through safe."

Constance was equally confident in her outlook. But she was upset when told a number of soothsayers were consulted to help trace her friend.

"My Catholic faith," she said, "does not allow for belief in human beings having supernatural powers."

"It's utter rubbish, poppy-cock!" she exploded, when told a medium had predicted that Jim was "safe but weak."

"My faith is in God," she reasoned, "and it is this faith in God that will see Jim through as well."

Chapter Nine

Dr. Ling arrived in Singapore on Thursday, March 30. Just after he reached home, he received a call from a man who identified himself as Michael Ian Vermont. He told Dr. Ling he had some information with regard to Jim's whereabouts. He asked if he could meet up with Dr. Ling to see if they could discuss the subject further. Without any hesitation, Dr. Ling agreed.

When he arrived at Dr. Ling's residence, the visitor seemed a bit nervous. After gaining his composure, he informed Dr. Ling that Jim was being kept at a house in Tapah. He added if Dr. Ling was prepared to accompany him to the municipality, the two of them could look into Jim's possible release.

Dr. Ling was for the idea but he was unable to go up to Tapah because of his work commitments. He suggested instead that Michael meet up with two of his other friends. Michael agreed. Before going off, Michael requested for some money. He told Dr. Ling he needed the money to travel up to Tapah. Out of goodwill, Dr. Ling gave him the equivalent of US$15.

Immediately after Michael had left, Dr. Ling called Helen and kept her informed of his meeting with Michael. Following this, Brigadier-General Edwin Black and Dean Frasche, two close friends of the Lings, were also kept informed. Both the general and Dean were for the idea of meeting up with Michael. But when they were at Tapah, Michael failed to show up. The next day, he called Helen and apologized to her for not being able to keep his appointment. While conversing with her, he suggested that another date be fixed. From the tone of his voice, Helen could sense "he was up to something which was no good." To satisfy her curiosity, she asked him for his name and Singaporean identification card number. He willingly gave them to her but a check with the authorities revealed there was no such person.

After this incident, "Michael" was neither heard of nor seen by the Lings. But it was only for "a short while." Some time later he surfaced again. This time round, he took on a more aggressive stance. He occasionally called them and reminded them to "get out of the country." He even threatened to burn down the shops owned by Helen Ling.

Initially, the Lings were troubled by his frequent threats. But as time slipped by, they learnt to take no notice of it.

Chapter Ten

Over at Tanah Rata, there was a noticeable change in mood as far as the scouting for Jim was concerned. The operation, which was then in its seventh day, began to gain momentum when it became apparent that Brigadier-General Edwin Black, the chief of the American support forces in Thailand, would be joining in the hunt.

Before coming over to the territory, the military leader kept in touch with a religious figure to ascertain if he could provide insights as to where Jim could be found. The soothsayer, a reasonably popular figure in Bangkok, did specify in one of his free-circulating pamphlets that:

> "Wishful thinking is the dowser's greatest enemy. If he is bent on finding water at a certain spot the pendulum will turn, the stick will pull down on that spot, and most probably he will be wrong in the prognostications.

> "Suppose a plane crashes between Rangoon and Bangkok, in the Tenasserim range — and that is a very bad place to crash — a good dowser will point out on the map the exact place where the plane is, and how many people still survive, and how many are wounded. It goes without saying that those indications may occasionally prove highly useful..."

Useful or not, General Black complied with whatever the clair-voyant requested. To make it easier for him, the general handed him a map of the resort. After taking a look at it, the mystic pointed to a spot and encouraged the commander to concentrate on the area which he had highlighted. Equipped with this information, General Black came to the retreat with his aide, Lieutenant Denis Horgan and his friend, Dean Frasche. The first thing they did was to visit the address where Jim had stayed. While they were at the double-storied house, Helen and Constance were asked about the developments which unfolded prior to the absence of their friend. Of the two, Constance had a lot more to say.

The three were told that before their coming over to stay with the Lings, Jim and Constance had spent a day in Penang. Since Jim was tied up with his work, it was Constance who took the trouble to finalize their travel arrangements.

When they met at Don Muang airport on Thursday, March 23, it became clear Jim was not in line with two statutory requirements. In the first instance, he had failed to get his compulsory cholera inocula-tion. Moreover, he had also forgotten to obtain his clearance certifi-cate to show he had no outstanding payments with the nation's income tax department. By right, he was not allowed to leave the country. Fortunately, Constance knew some of the officials rather well and this helped to smoothen out Jim's irregularities.

The couple left Bangkok as planned and got in to Penang in the afternoon. She recalled that "neither of us had been there before and we were anxious to see the island (for ourselves)." She added: "We hired a car and (while) driving around the island… Jim became anxious to have a haircut." Constance admitted she was put off with Jim's unexpected request. She dropped him off at a barber shop while they were on their way to the Ambassador Hotel.

When Jim got back, Constance remembered him commenting that it would have been better if they had stayed at the Eastern & Oriental hotel. He felt the E & O had much the same feel as the Oriental in Bangkok. Constance was unable to make out why he brought this up. She never did ask him and it was left as that.

Later that day, the two of them had a quiet dinner at an Indian restaurant, after which they went for an evening stroll. The subsequent morning they got up early, booked a taxi and made their way to the province. While they were on their way to the mainland, the driver of the taxi suddenly stopped his vehicle and left them for about five minutes. He later returned with a relief driver who took over the driving from him.

Apart from this, they also encountered another change just before they got over to the prefecture. This happened at Tapah where they not only had to deal with a change of drivers but a change of vehicles as well. The next taxi which they were told to board had two Chinese passengers waiting in it. Jim and Constance were totally against the idea of sharing their ride with the other two commuters. After some deliberation, the other two travelers were asked to get off and the driver saw to it that they were driven on their own to Moonlight.

Satisfied with Constance's recollections, General Black and his crew got together to work out their plan for the next day.

The following morning, the threesome got up early and made the necessary arrangements for an aerial tower to be positioned on a water tank near the house. The device was designed to throw a radar communication 'net' which covered a radius of approximately sixteen kilometers. Lieutenant Horgan was put in charge of the tower and his role was to ensure that a minute-by-minute radio contact was established with his superior's exploration team.

General Black, who was equipped with a portable wireless set, went into the forest to conduct a survey of his own. He was in constant contact with his aide while being accompanied by Dean and two aborigines. Apart from being able to keep in touch with his assistant, General Black was also able to establish radio contact with the other parties who were on the hunt for Jim.

The search conducted on Saturday, April 1, was indeed extensive. Joining in the exploration were two hundred more officers and men from Perak's police field force. They were earlier engaged in a training operation at Tambun near Ipoh. They came to the hill station from Tanjung Rambutan after making their way through the woods. They were later ordered to merge with the various parties who were based at Tanah Rata.

Just before the lunch break, a twelve-year-old boy who knew where Jim could be found came forward to share his knowledge with the police. Mustada bin Yahaya, a *kramat hidup* (living spirit) told the police that Jim had moved from the state of Pahang to the neighboring state of Kelantan. He said through his father, Yahaya bin Ahmad Hashim, 63, that it was pointless to look for Jim at the enclave. His father, a farmer, informed the police his son's services were strictly voluntary. He added that the subject of money would not be discussed unless Jim was discovered based on his son's revelation.

The police, however, did not pay much attention to the boy's observations. After the lunch break, the area near Moonlight was backtracked. The sweep of the wasteland was later extended to the hamlet's north and northeast. By late evening, most of the assigned parties were back at their post. Throughout their mission, they came across no sign of Jim.

The next day, there was no let up in their pursuit of Jim: the police carried on combing the area from where they had earlier left off; General Black and his crew went about with a separate probe of their own. The Sunday exploration, though intensive, proved to be no more of a success.

On the third day, General Black and his party informed the police they were calling off their investigations. They left the scene and got over to Kuala Lumpur the same day. While resting at the Malaysian capital, the commander told a group of reporters that "there has been absolutely no trace of Jim's whereabouts." "Jim," he reasoned, "has knowledge of jungle survival. This would have enabled him to survive for a few days. On realizing he was lost, he would have been on the lookout for a stream. He would have subsequently followed it expecting to come to a village.

"I find his disappearance rather strange. There has not been a single clue, not a bit of torn clothing or even a shoe. According to the police, a ransom is usually demanded within a time frame of forty-eight hours. Nothing of that sort has surfaced since the day he went missing."

That said, General Black and Dean returned to Bangkok. As for Lieutenant Horgan, it is believed he stayed in Kuala Lumpur before heading back for the United States.

Meanwhile, at Moonlight, Helen and Constance, both of whom had extended their stay, left the area for Singapore. Helen was especially thankful to the authorities for assigning Inspector Tan Ai Bee to look after Constance and her. She was also grateful to the police for doing their best to locate Jim.

After their departure on April 5, there was no slowdown in the probe for Jim. The police went on with their hunt. A party comprising fifty men left Tanah Rata and headed more than eight kilometers into the jungle. Two air force helicopters were also on hand to assist them in their pursuit. Still, there were no signs of Jim.

In the afternoon, a nine-man team led by businessman Yip Wah Swee entered the woods to conduct an investigation of their own. They were determined to find for Jim at a particular hill. Before heading for the vicinity, Wah Swee told two reporters he had met a 'higher medium' from Bidor, Perak. The soothsayer informed him that Jim was still alive and he could be detected on a knoll which is not far from where he stayed. According to Wah Swee, the seer notified him that, "Jim is on top of a hill from which all the parties had turned their backs after checking its foot." He was told to go up to the summit and bring him down. But before doing so, it was required of him to fire two packets of firecrackers. The purpose was to scare away the spirits who were residing in the area.

Wah Swee had tremendous faith in whatever the mystic had instructed him to do. On reaching the site, he and the members of his group fired two packets of firecrackers. After the smoke had cleared, they eagerly made their way to the top. When they reached the peak, their excitement turned into disappointment: Jim was not to be found. Crestfallen, all nine got off from the mount.

Chapter Eleven

The pursuit for Jim went on uninterruptedly for eleven days. On their part, the police did put in a concerted effort to search for him. On the twelfth day, there was a change in their operation: more than two hundred officers and men were ordered to head back to their base in Perak. Only a force numbering less than a hundred was instructed to stay behind.

Over in Thailand, the situation was a lot different. The Thai Silk Company, which was monitoring developments closely, announced that the US$10,000 reward for the finder of Jim would be raised by another US$2,500. George Barrie, Jim's business associate, was the one who came up with the offer.

Jim or no Jim, the Thai Silk Company went on to function in much the same way as it previously did. In an interview with the press, Charles U. Sheffield said, "Until we hear from him, we will just continue producing and selling silk the way we've always done. There is no doubt we would not be able to find someone to replace him as a designer. He has been into designing for fifteen years. Some of his designs are classics and some of these are still being sold today.

"If he does not turn up we would have no choice but to find another designer to replace him. He would have to be someone who has much the same feel as Jim. Whatever the outcome, there would not be much of a change in the overall policy of the company. For the time being, we do not want to make any quick changes in the company's general set-up. We believe there is still a good possibility that he will be found."

The clueless search continued. For days the jungles were traversed. Cries of "Jim! Jim!" drew no response. With the dwindling of the police field force, the casting about for him took on a different twist – the seekers narrowed down to two categories: the first were experts who knew the place like the back of their hands; the second were those who delved into the supernatural. Both parties were just as confident of success; they were more than eager to track Jim down.

The first to do so was Awan bin Osman. He went into the woods on the morning of Thursday, April 20. A few hours later, he emerged from the wasteland. When sought for his observations, the *bomoh* (witch doctor) was quick to say that Jim "did not go into the tangled vegetation." He confessed that while he was in no man's land, he managed to come into contact with a *raja kramat* (spirit king). The supernatural being informed him it was pointless for him to look for Jim in the wilderness. He later told a group of reporters he needed more time to reflect on the kind of situation Jim was in. A week slipped by. Then two. After that, nothing more was heard of from him.

On Sunday, April 23, Richard Noone, 49, a British officer with the Southeast Asia Treaty Organization came onto the scene. He was no stranger to the jungles of the area. At one stage, he served as head of the Malayan Department of Aborigines.

After two days of planning, Richard, a Cambridge-trained anthropologist, went into the woodland with two assistants. Both helpers were equally at home in any tropical rainforest: one was a border scout from Sarawak; the other was an aborigine witch doctor. While they were in the wilds, they met a few aborigines but they were unable to provide the threesome with leads as to where Jim could be found. Undiscouraged, the group carried on exploring in the hope of meeting up with him from where the field force had earlier left off.

While Richard and his two partners were still in the green quietude, a controversial figure showed up at Tanah Rata. He was none other than Peter Hurkos, a private investigator from the United States. He came to the haven on Tuesday, April 25 with his personal secretary, Miss Stephany Farb (now Mrs. Stephany Hurkos) and Lieutenant Denis Horgan.

While the three of them were at the resort, Peter took the opportunity to make his extrasensory powers known. He told some members of the police interesting things about their lives. A young officer, for instance, was told that prior to his reporting for duty, he made love to his wife on a kitchen table. Peter's clairvoyance turned out to be correct.

As for the circumstances that Jim was in, Peter was sure he had an answer. While he was at the mansion, the first thing he did was to pace the garden in an unusual manner. Then he stopped to feel a chair which was left at the veranda. After a short pause, he gave out a loud yell, "This is the chair! Yes, this is the chair that Jim sat on just before he disappeared!" A brief silence followed. A few minutes later, he sat on the floor just outside the house. A photograph of Jim and two maps were laid out. The first chart highlighted the countries of Asia; the second featured the details of the retreat. While glancing at Jim's photograph, his face grew tensed. Seconds later he broke out into a stammer. According to his secretary, he uttered the following string of words:

"He was sitting in the chair... right over there... he was not sitting in the house... the chair was on the veranda... aagh, Prebi, ooogh... Thompson... Prebi, Pridi... fourteen people... fourteen people took

him... Prebe or Bebe... orah blah-lun-dah Bebe... he is not in the jungle... I want to follow the route where they picked him up... he was sitting right there... this chair... there was nobody in the room... they were upstairs... he was sitting outside in this chair... this chair... not in the jungle... car... fourteen people... one vehicle, like a military vehicle... like a truck... I see truck... ah, truck, about from here on the road... he walks down the road... somebody woke him up... he was sitting outside and somebody came in here... a friend of his... Bebe or Prebie... Pridi has own army... no bandits... nothing to do with bandits... he walks about half a mile, with Bebe or Prebie... truck on the road... fourteen people... one person here, one person picked him up... he knows him... he was sitting on the veranda and the men came in... asked for something, I don't know... he went down the road... got chloroform... chloroform... sleep in truck..."

After returning to his normal self, Peter stated, "it is ridiculous to look for Jim at the Highlands or even within a-hundred-and-sixty kilometer radius of it."

"There is no way you'll find him there," he declared. "It's just that he had been abducted to another country. You can take it from me he is not being held for ransom. I am prepared to stake my neck on this!"

Peter was positive fourteen members of an underground communist movement took Jim away after knocking him out with chloroform. Jim, he claimed, met a man in civilian clothes while he was sitting at the veranda. He got up to greet the man. A while later, the two of them left the residence and took a walk down the road. After clearing a distance of about a kilometer, Jim was rendered unconscious with a dose of chloroform. Immediately after this, thirteen men dressed in military attire came out of their hiding places and carried him to a truck. Within minutes, he was transferred to a nearby river where a boat brought him to another state. Much later, his kidnappers saw to it that he was smuggled into Cambodia.

After completing his assessment, Peter left the scene and flew in to Bangkok where he met up with a Buddhist monk named Keo. During their encounter, they were in agreement Jim was held in Cambodia for political reasons. Before their meeting came to an end, the Thai mystic predicted Jim would come out in the open and have something to say about the war in Vietnam. He envisaged this would take place on or before June 15.

After his get-together with Keo, Peter and his secretary left the country for the United States. Prior to their heading for Bangkok, Peter was asked by several parties as to how he acquired his talent for extra-sensory perception. To satisfy their curiosity he said, "I am a Christian (Roman Catholic). My work as a telepathy expert has nothing to do with showmanship. It is a gift from God."

But while he was at the refuge, he left one aspect of his stammering unanswered, that is, the similar sounding names of Prebi and Pridi. Many who were keeping tabs on Peter's visionary recapitulation took it that he was obviously referring to Pridi Panomyong, the ex-Prime Minister of Thailand.

There is no doubt Pridi was a colorful figure in Thai politics. In 1932, during a *coup d'etat*, Pridi was appointed to serve as the People's Party's chief driving force. Around that time, the worldwide economic crisis had a considerable effect on Thailand's rice exports. To correct the unfavorable situation, King Prajadhipok, was persuaded by his council of advisers to drop the gold standard which linked the Thai baht to the British pound. But, by the time he did so, the country's financial situation took a turn for the worse. The government was then left with not much of a choice but to reduce the wages of its junior staff members. This led to widespread discontentment. For the next few months, rumors were rampant that King Prajadhipok would be the last regal representative of Thailand. In April 1932, he presided over the grand pageantry which featured a royal barge procession in Bangkok. Two months later, a *coup d'etat* brought his paternal but absolute rule to an end. The coup was staged by the People's Party which was made up of representatives from the military and a number of civilians.

On the military side, Captain Luang Pibulsongram (Pibul) managed to garner the support of the army to form a separate political front of his own. With a few tanks, he initiated a 'revolution' which subsequently led to the 'capture' of the city. Apart from this, he also succeeded in holding several members of the royal family as hostages.

At the time of the 'uprising', King Prajadhipok was not in his homeland. When news of the coup reached him, he quickly returned to Bangkok. To avoid a scene of carnage, he accepted the provisional constitution by which he "ceased to rule but continued to reign." This marked the end of absolute monarchy in Thailand; it was now replaced by party dictatorship.

Once in power, the administration was quick to assert the locals were not educated enough to rule themselves. In essence, the incoming government's first ten years of rule was to be taken as a trial period for democracy to be introduced into the country. In December 1932, King Prajadhipok was made to sign a newly enacted Parliamentary Constitution which called for a general election to be held once in every four years.

A year later, the administration became divided by Pridi's style of government which advocated the nationalization of all land under cultivation. His policy was viewed by many as being typically communistic and this forced him out of office. The following year, a counter-coup took place and this brought about a reshuffling of the members in the Executive Council during which Pibul gained ascendancy. For the next twenty years, Thai politics was dominated by either Pibul or Pridi. Pibul, who became a general, had the backing of the military; Pridi, on the other hand, had the support of the nation's intelligentsia.

While power see-sawed between Pibul and Pridi, King Prajadhipok found his new role increasingly uncomfortable. His differences with the regime resulted in his abdication of the throne in 1935. When he died in 1941, Ananda Mahidol, his ten-year-old nephew, was proclaimed king. A Regency Council was formed and Pridi was appointed to serve as regent to the young king who was studying in Switzerland at that time.

For the next three years, the country had to put up with a series of political upheavals. Pibul took advantage of the uneasy situation to strengthen his control over the country.

A few years later, a pro-Allied underground resistance group, the *Seri Thai* or Free Thai Movement, emerged. During the Japanese Occupation, it received the full support of Pridi who was then regent to King Ananda. The group was trained in Sri Lanka with the aim of carrying out clandestine activities against the Japanese. When the Japanese surrendered in 1945, Pibul's collaborative government collapsed. Seni Pramoj, a politician based in the United States, was appointed to serve as Prime Minister. But his premiership did not last for long. A few months later, Pridi took over. That same year, King Ananda returned to Thailand. A year later, the young king was reportedly shot dead while he was in his room. Many took it that Pridi had a hand in the crime. To avoid getting himself into any trouble, he left the country.

There was one theory which cropped up concerning Peter's mentioning of Pridi. Many were of the impression that it was Pridi who met Jim while he was sitting at the veranda. After an exchange of words, both of them left the house and made their way to the main road. After covering a distance of about a kilometer, Pridi knocked him out with a dose of chloroform. Following this, thirteen men came out of their hiding places and carried him to a waiting truck. Being a Sunday, Pridi instructed the driver to avoid the busier roads. The under-utilized roads to the golf course were used instead. Pridi then saw to it that Jim was put on a boat and brought over to a safe place. He then made arrangements for Jim to be sneaked out of the country.

But why did Pridi have to do such a thing? The common opinion was that Pridi was anxious to make a political comeback. He had no one else to turn to but Jim. When he brought this up to Jim, Jim was against the idea. Fearing that Jim would leak his plans, Pridi took no chances, knocked Jim out with chloroform, and later saw to it that Jim was got rid off.

In the Thai scheme of things, many accepted this theory for what it was made out to be. When approached by the press, Pridi denied being involved in such an entanglement. To prove his point, he produced documentary proof to show he was never in Malaysia.

When this theory lost favor, another speculation took center stage. A number of pressmen were of the view that a communist agent met Jim while he was sitting at the veranda. The communist leader, who was known to him, approached him and asked him to accompany him down the road. While the two of them were taking a walk, the leader injected him with a portion of chloroform. Within minutes, Jim became unconscious. He was then put into a military truck and brought to a riverbank where a vessel was used to transfer him to another state. It was here that Chin Peng, the former head of the outlawed Communist Party of Malaya, took custody of him. When the time was right, he saw to it that Jim was flown in to Cambodia. While in Cambodia, the plan was for Jim to be brainwashed and used by the communists to exert pressure on the Americans. In the late 1960s, the war in Vietnam was reaching its climax. The Americans used Thailand as a springboard to launch their air attacks on Hanoi. To put a check on this advantage, the communists had to think of a way of outsmarting the Americans. Launching a full-scale military attack on Thailand made no sense. A better option was to make use of Jim. He was to be progressively branded as a defector. An ongoing campaign on his demerits was to follow. Given his background as a spy, the Thai government would be cornered into a situation for knowingly closing an eye on his covert activities. Over time, it would be forced to come up with some compromise to appease the communists. What the communists were hoping for was that Thailand would shut down all the American bases on its soil. By doing so, the Americans would be deprived of a military outpost just outside the Indo-China war zone.

Most pressmen were also suspicious that the Central Intelligence Agency (CIA) was well aware of this ploy. When queried, the CIA opted to downplay the issue. This caused greater suspicion. The press began to speculate the CIA could have been engaged in a series of behind-the-scene negotiations with the communists. This was the prognosis: the CIA pressed for Jim's release in return for favorable concessions. But the communists were not keen to let Jim go as they were unhappy with the dispensations that came their way. Hoping for something better, the communists held on to him.

But what did Peter actually mean when he said that Jim had been abducted to another country but "is not being held for ransom"?

The commonly held reasoning was that the communists were frustrated they could not make use of Jim to fulfill their political cause. If he was portrayed as a defector, few people would have believed it. The CIA was well aware of this fact. Not to be outdone, the communists came up with a different arrangement – they kept Jim to help develop their silk industry

To a limited extent, some found this theory to be somewhat acceptable. But there were many who felt otherwise. Quite a few, however, preferred to be more diplomatic about their views: they chose instead to classify Peter's theory as "interesting." Richard Noone was one such person. When told of Peter's prognosis, Richard had this to say: "If what Peter says is true, then it makes the search for Jim all the more interesting."

In a way, he was right.

Chapter Twelve

On Wednesday, April 26, Richard Noone and his two assistants, Rahim bin Kamman and Toh Pawang Angah Sidek, emerged from the forest. In all, they spent a total of thirty-six hours looking for Jim.

"I am fully convinced," Richard told a group of reporters, "that Jim isn't in the jungle. We went further into the woods, starting off from where the police field force men had earlier left off. But we could not find any clue which could be of use in leading us to him.

"During our survey, we came across a steep cliff. We had to turn back. I don't think it would have been possible for Jim at his age to have scaled that cliff. Furthermore, I don't think he would have gone as far as we went if he did go into the wilderness."

When told of Peter's visit and his abduction theory, Richard expressed his surprise at the soothsayer's claim that Jim had been kidnapped and was being held as a captive.

"Telepathy," he admitted, "is something new to me. If what Peter says is true, then it makes the search for Jim all the more interesting."

To a considerable extent, Richard was right. The departure of Jim did create a high level of interest. In Bangkok, for instance, the Thai Silk Company continued to observe the mystery of his eclipse with great concern. Charles U. Sheffield, the acting manager of the company, declared that their earlier reward for the finder of Jim had been doubled from US$12,500 to US$25,000. This incentive did help to generate a higher level of interest in Jim's status. But this was not the only reward which was made known at this time. In a separate announcement, a group of Jim's friends came up with a different enticement. They made it clear they were willing to sacrifice US$10,000 to anyone who was able to provide them with proof of Jim's death. To a large degree, both offers highlighted the fact that those who knew him well were indeed worried for him. The same could also be said of the Malaysian police. In early May, it announced it had turned to Interpol for help. This was disclosed by Perak's officer-in-charge of criminal investigation, Assistant Commissioner U. Santokh Singh. He described the request of the police in seeking Interpol's assistance as a "routine matter." He went on to say the police had not given up on Jim. "The hunt," he added, "will continue and investigations into his sudden disappearance are still proceeding." He informed the public there had been no change to the RM10,000 reward for information leading to Jim's whereabouts. He encouraged those who held any clue to Jim's actual circumstances to make a report at any police station. On its part, he stated, the police would see to it that whatever leads that came its way would be attended to accordingly.

Chapter Thirteen

The loss of Jim was absolutely puzzling. Many were stirred to come up with their own conclusions. One such speculation was that while he was in the jungle, Jim came into contact with an aborigine girl. After a brief acquaintance, he went ahead and married her.

An Iban, when told of this reasoning, considered it hard to accept. He said, "Such a development is unlikely to have happened. What could have possibly unfolded is this: while he was trying to find his way through the forest, he could have been spotted by an aborigine. I suppose the native must have made use of his blowpipe and blew a dart straight into him."

A mind reader, who declined to be named, did not think that this was likely the case. He alleged that Jim was like an old elephant. Jim, he sensed, was well aware it was "more or less time for him to die. To die in the city of Bangkok made no sense to him. The impenetrable vegetation of the Malaysian 'alps' seemed more appropriate. So on Sunday, March 26, when the Lings were in their bedroom and his friend Constance was in another room, he quietly left the house and made his way for the woods. While he was in no man's land, he kept on walking for as long as his legs could carry him. A few days later, he collapsed and died."

A Caucasian lady, however, made it out to be otherwise. She confessed she was informed by "a reliable source that Jim was run down by a truck while he was heading for the main road. On realizing he had done wrong, the driver quickly dumped Jim's body into the rear of his vehicle and later saw to it that it was disposed of quietly."

A lawyer, when informed about this speculation, took it to be "a little out of this world." Based on reports he read of in the press, George Ramasamy was sure Jim did not go into the jungle. "If he had done so," he continued, "he would have been found."

"Jim," he reasoned, "was not a stupid person. He must have been in some difficulty which he perceived as hard to overcome. Such being the case, he had to pretend he was going for a holiday. Along the way, he vanished from the scene."

Agreeing with the lawyer, an ex-serviceman from the Intelligence Unit of the Malaysian Armed Forces adduced that "it is obvious Jim shrewdly took a side trip without keeping anyone informed. That is why there was no ransom pertaining to his likely whereabouts."

When quizzed about Jim's exit, Alan Lim Tiong Hwa came up with a different interpretation. The late correspondent disclosed that "when Jim came to the Highlands, many took it he was coming over for a holiday. But few were aware the resort was actually the gateway for his drug business.

"Yes, Jim was involved in drugs. When he first came to Thailand, he saw the potential for making a fortune out of dealing with drugs. He knew if he had gone into the trade, it wouldn't be long before the authorities would come after him. The best way out was to establish a decent business to serve as a front for whatever plans he had for his future dealings in drugs. By doing so, the odds of his being caught would be narrowed down to a considerable extent.

"From the way he conducted himself, many took it he was connected with silk. But Jim was not only synonymous with silk; he was also associated with drugs in a big way. For years he was suspected as being one of the many drug lords of the Golden Triangle. To the best of my knowledge, he is the only person who got along well with all the leaders in Indochina. How did he manage it? Simple… he had both the money and the resources to do just this. Just as much as he needed them, they in return needed him as well. He needed them to police his drug business; on their part, they needed him to see the fulfillment of their political cause."

The ex-pressman went on to say that Jim's set-up was not as complex as what one would make it out to be. According to him, the drugs were periodically brought into the country from across the Thai-Malaysian border. He added, "The boundary line at that time was loosely guarded. Jim cleverly capitalized on this drawback and saw to it that the drugs were brought over to the province via a track which terminates at Ringlet.

"It is a fact Jim was no stranger to Foster's Lakehouse (now The Lakehouse). It was from here he saw the overall distribution of his drugs.

"I believe there are two reasons as to why he went missing. In the first instance, he could have deceived the members of his syndicate, taking a vast sum of money. The other could be the long arm of the law was now closing in on him. Of the two, the former seems to be more in line."

Having said that, how then did Jim manage to depart from the haven without leaving a single trace behind?

"He discreetly made his way for Ringlet," confided the correspondent. "It was from here," he observed, "that he took one of the tracks which ensured his exit out of the retreat."

While some were comfortable with whatever the late journalist had had to say, there were many others who were not in agreement with him. A religious leader, for example, took it that "Jim was living in bondage." Eventually," he said, "the Lord had to deal with him the hard way."

A number of Thais, however, were of the conviction that he could have positioned a newly acquired image in an entirely wrong area of his house. This act of carelessness, they sensed, could have brought about much anguish to the idol in question. To teach him a lesson, the spirit made him go round in circles. Being stubborn, he chose not to repent. It was because of this, they reasoned, he has continued to remain lost all this while.

Apart from the Thais, the Malaysians too had their own views: it ranged from his being "kidnapped" to his "slipping and falling into an animal trap."

Across the Causeway, most Singaporeans were of the impression that Jim could have gone off course "as a result of losing his sense of direction." They felt "if he could get his bearing right, he should be able to find his way back in no time at all."

When asked for his assessment, an ex-Rover scout agreed with this line of thinking. He acknowledged the outpost has long been noted for its intricate network of tracks. Paths 4, 9, 11 and 12, he observed, are suitable for family strolls. Paths 3, 5, 7 and 10 require a much longer walk. As for paths 2 and 8, he was prepared to classify them as "comparatively steep." He added that "although most of the trails are moderately short, there is still the possibility of combining a few routes to create an interesting walk. An example would be the combination of paths 2, 3 and 8.

"If Jim had taken this route at 4.30 pm, he would have been back by 7.30pm. It is unfortunate he did not do so. I think he could have left one of the paths along the way. While drifting into the forest, he could have ended up being disorientated. For a moment, he could have been in a situation where he just did not know what to do. The first option was to backtrack; the second was to continue on from wherever he was. Of the two, I suppose, he must have opted for the latter. This was so because time was no longer on his side. He knew if he had chosen to make an about turn, he would not have been able to return before sunset. The best option was for him to carry on from wherever he was. While he was in such a situation, he had to depend on his jungle knowledge to see him through whatever difficulties he was in. Sad to say, this did not turn out to be the case."

Asked for his opinion, Dr. Ling stated it is a fact that Jim "was by nature an adventurous person. (It is common knowledge) he had a particular interest in wild plants." He felt it was more these two factors than anything else that could have "carried him further into the woods."

A plantation owner did not think that this was necessarily the case. He said: "I have lived here all my life. This place is noted for its wild animals. I'm sure Jim was attacked by a tiger."

Alan Tan, however, saw things differently. The ex-banker was sure Jim had a motive for going into the woodland.

"Jim," he felt, "was actually hard pressed for cash. He needed the money to finance his company's new building. His only asset was his famed 'House on the Klong'. If he had mortgaged it, it would have been indicative he was in bad shape.

"To come out of this sorry situation, he made up his mind to take his own life.

"It did not take him long to work out an arrangement. The emphasis was on simplicity. The first thing he did was to head for the Lutheran Mission bungalow. He stopped there for a while. Once he was sure he was seen, he left the place.

"He was now free to do whatever he had planned to do. Best of all, he committed suicide without leaving any traces behind."

Siva, a popular guide at the center, considered Alan's conclusion rather unacceptable. "It's ridiculous," he asserted, "that Jim went into the wasteland to commit suicide.

"I have lived here for more than forty years of my life. I can safely say if Jim had commit suicide, his remains would have been found.

"The timberland out here is unlike any other: for decades, it has been home to thousands of people. These people know the place like the back of their hands. If anyone were to collapse and die in their backyard, they would be the first to know of it. In time to come, the authorities too would be made aware of such an eventuality."

Siva was not alone in his reasoning. Dr. Ammundsen, Constance and Dean were also in agreement that Jim did not come over to the area to end his life.

Dr. Ammundsen was positive Jim "was a man (who was) very interested in his work. I don't think there was anything in his mental outlook which would make him do a thing like that."

Constance, on the other hand, was sure Jim "was looking forward to going back to Bangkok."

"He was a tired man," she said, "that is why he came here for a holiday."

Dean, who was with Jim the night before he left Bangkok, was affirmative he saw no signs of depression in him.

"Jim," he observed, "is a very stable individual. It is unlikely of him to have taken his own life."

If Jim did not commit suicide, what then could have possibly happened to him while he was at the enclave? Some of his friends felt he could have been kidnapped while he was alone. They did state he got to know too many communists during his lifetime. They were sure the communists with whom he was acquainted were the ones who actually abducted him.

One spin on this theory was that a convoy of five cars was seen going up the holiday center before Jim went astray. The five cars were later seen coming down the road after he was proclaimed as missing.

Many who were keeping tabs on the saga of Jim's disappearance were prepared to accept the fact he was kidnapped by an organized gang. But there was a funny twist to the described episode: of the thousands who were at "Cameron's Land", only one person remembered seeing a convoy of five cars with Thai license plates plying up and down the haunt. An investigation by the Malaysian police revealed that such an event never did take place. Since that be so, the sighting of the attendant must be the imagination of one man more than anything else. However, there was a separate development which did not go unnoticed: on the day of Jim's eclipse, two limousines were spotted at Tapah. A while later, both vehicles were seen heading for the hill station. The two cars were later seen driving past Tapah after Jim was reported as lost.

On the international front, many believed it was the Chinese government who had had a hand in bringing Jim under their shadow. For a number of years, the Chinese silk industry was hard hit by the quality silk which was being produced by Thailand. The Chinese, however, did not publicize it for fear of losing face. To outdo the Thais, the Chinese came up with a plan whereby Jim had to leave Thailand for Malaysia. While he was in Malaysia he was to create the impression he was there for a holiday. When it was time for him to leave, the arrangements would then be made for him to fly in to China. Once in China, he was to see to it that their ailing industry was revived. To get him to do just this, it is deemed the Chinese government arranged a transfer of US$1 million to a foreign bank which was based in Bangkok. Many assumed Jim withdrew the money prior to his coming over to Malaysia.

Perceived or real, the topic of Jim's obliteration from the scene continued to grow with each and every passing day. The speculations that emerged led many to believe he could either be in Malaysia or Cambodia. Why not China? Many took it that the Chinese silk industry was long established before the arrival of Marco Polo. Why then, debunkers argued, should the Chinese be dependent on Jim when they knew the trade inside out?

Jim Thompson, the Thai Silk king

Lutheran Mission home

Sunlight villa

Moonlight bungalow

All Souls' Church

Che Fatimah
the maid who saw Jim

Dr. Dadi Balsara
the Indian astrologer

Richard Noone
the British anthropologist

Mrs. Mangskau
Jim's social companion

Lt. Denis Horgan
the aide to Gen. Black

Dr. Ling Tien Gi
the owner of Moonlight villa

Gen. Edwin Black
the American commander

Mrs. Helen Ling
Jim's long-time friend

Peter Hurkos
the Dutch telepathy expert

Pridi Panomyong
the ex-Thai Prime Minister

Gunung Brinchang Radio & TV station

Tanah Rata in the 1960s

Jim Thompson (in white shirt) circa 1961

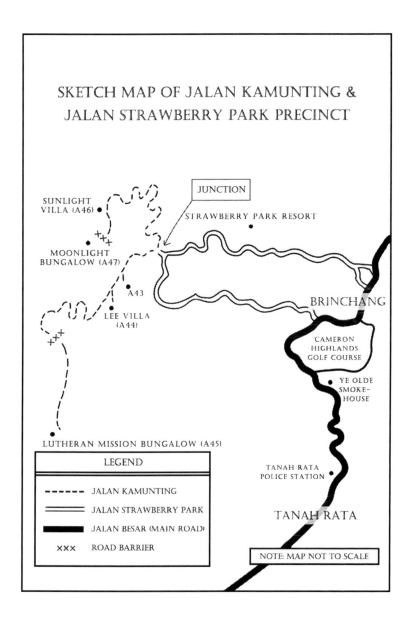

SKETCH MAP OF JALAN KAMUNTING &
JALAN STRAWBERRY PARK PRECINCT

JUNCTION

SUNLIGHT
VILLA (A46)

STRAWBERRY PARK RESORT

MOONLIGHT
BUNGALOW (A47)

A43

BRINCHANG

LEE VILLA
(A44)

CAMERON
HIGHLANDS
GOLF COURSE

YE OLDE
SMOKE-
HOUSE

LUTHERAN MISSION BUNGALOW (A45)

LEGEND

------- JALAN KAMUNTING

====== JALAN STRAWBERRY PARK

▬▬▬▬ JALAN BESAR (MAIN ROAD)

×××   ROAD BARRIER

TANAH RATA
POLICE STATION

TANAH RATA

NOTE: MAP NOT TO SCALE

Chapter Fourteen

The last appearance of Jim was unique in many ways: for the next few weeks, his fading away was not only discussed at length; equally interesting, it became a subject which refused to die off on its own.

While many were trying to figure things out, an odd development surfaced about five months after he vanished. This incident not only threw up a lot of questions; it also affixed a fresh dimension to his strange exit from the retreat.

On Wednesday, August 30, it was reported that his older sister, Mrs. Katherine Thompson Wood, 74, was found dead in her Pennsylvania home. The police were of the opinion a blunt object was used to carry out the murder. But they were positive her death had no connection to Jim's departure from the refuge. While some were inclined to accept it as such, there were many who were not at all prepared to do so. What was it that made them doubtful? At the outset, the police mentioned the motive for her murder had nothing to do with robbery. Since that be the case, why then was she killed? Moreover, why did her two dogs remain silent while she was being attacked? Were her dogs afraid of the murderer or was it that they knew the killer?

Whatever it is, the commonly held reasoning was the assassin was trying to get something out of her. Unable to do so, she was clobbered to death.

For quite some time, many took it that the CIA had a hand in her assassination. Later, it was also speculated that the involvement of the communists was not to be ruled out altogether.

The murder of Jim's sister not only left many in want of an answer; it also added fuel to a new round of speculation. Most of Jim's friends were of the view there was a link between her death and his disappearance from the Cameron Highlands. But they realized it was hard to prove the two events were, in all probability, connected to one another. As such, they had no choice but to hold on to their observations until further evidence was made available.

Just as the speculations were about to die off, an interesting character came onto the scene. He was Robert McGowan, an ex-major from the British army. He told a group of Jim's friends he had seen Jim in a vision. He claimed Jim was imprisoned in Cambodia and that he could be located in a double-storied house in the district of Stung Treng. He went on to say that outside the home was a wooden wheel. According to him, the wheel was "leaning close to the entrance of the dwelling."

At first, Robert was made out to be another quack. It was only after he drove down the streets of Bangkok blindfolded that his words were taken seriously. It was alleged that a group of Jim's friends later got together to organize a rescue mission of their own. To add punch to their operation, they recruited the services of an ex-Gurkha. Their arrangement was to leave Thailand for Cambodia in an airplane. On nearing Stung Treng, the pilot was to create the impression the aircraft was encountering some mechanical problem. On landing, all were to pay attention to the described structure. Once spotted, the Gurkha was to burst into the unit and rescue Jim. He was to ensure that Jim was immediately brought over to the 'stalled' plane. After this was done, they were to head back for Thailand.

While their scheme was being hatched, the CIA somehow came to know of it. On the day the group was supposed to leave, a few agency officials met up with them and advised them to do away with their plan. For the next few days, they felt rather dejected that their mission had had to be abandoned. But deep inside them, they were not keen to see it end just like that. A few weeks later, a handful of them got together and arranged for the Gurkha to cross into Cambodia. He spent a fortnight in Stung Treng. While moving around, he came across a number of two-storied houses – none of them had a wheel leaning against it.

Chapter Fifteen

The casting about for Jim did not end at Stung Treng: it, in fact, marked the extension of more searches in other areas as well. Most of the investigations, if not all, were carried out in earnest. But the groups that went out of their way to look for him were in no way successful in their effort to find him. A good example was a Japanese team who crossed the Thai border town of Ban Aranyaprathet in 1968. After spending a week in the communities of Siem Pang and Virachei, they came to the conclusion that Jim was not to be found in Cambodia.

What was it that made them want to head that way? At one stage, there was a rumor in the Thai capital that Jim was being held captive in the northeastern part of Cambodia. Later, it was believed if he was not being detained in Stung Treng, then he could be at either Siem Pang or Virachei. The Japanese, who were told of the failed attempt at Stung Treng, decided to give the other two municipalities a try. But their hope of coming into contact with him turned out to be a disappointment.

After this endeavor, there were three other events which helped to bring about a fair measure of excitement in nailing down his likely whereabouts. The first was a report of his being sighted on the Thai beach resort of Ko Samui. Later, it was discovered the Caucasian who resembled Jim was not him; he was in fact a German who was enjoying a long stay on the island.

The next development which hinted at the possibility that Jim was still alive was an alleged photograph of him which was featured in a now-defunct tabloid. It depicted him in the company of four Asian-looking men. In the picture, all five were in the process of sharing a meal. They had a bowl (of rice?) in one hand and a pair of chopsticks in the other. The picture gave the impression he was going through much hardship and difficulty. He, like the rest, was portrayed as having to squat to have his meal. Later, it was confirmed the Caucasian was not Jim – he was actually an American who was captured by the Laotians at the height of the Vietnam War.

The other episode which caught the imagination of many involved an Indian mystic by the name of Dr. Dadi Balsara. He informed the press he came to have an interest in Jim's predicament as a result of reading about it in the newspapers. He said a few days after Jim was reported as lost, he drew out Jim's 'astrological chart' to see if the 'stars' could provide him with a clue as to where Jim could be found. From the chart, it became clear to him that Jim was alive and abducted for personal reasons.

"Astrology," he declared, "is not to be sneered at. It is a study of cosmic cycles of facts accumulated through millennia. The positioning of the stars at a particular moment decides the future of the events taking place at that moment of time."

While he was in Bangkok, Dr. Balsara got to know some people who were close to Jim. In getting to know them, he was not only brought over to Jim's house; equally noteworthy, he was also extended the privilege of lying down on Jim's bed. Whether his senses were alerted to anything or not, he chose not to disclose it in the open. Much later, it became evident he was really of not much of a help. At the end of it all, he left the scene and nothing more has been heard of from him ever since.

After the unfolding of these events, the hunt for Jim slowly came to a close. Finally, the painful news had to be made known: a Thai court, at the request of some of his family members, went ahead and pronounced him dead. The declaration was made in early 1974, that is, exactly seven years after he disappeared.

It could be acknowledged the decision of the court caught many by surprise. For the next few months his fate was hotly debated in a number of places. But the answers that emerged generally led no one anywhere.

Chapter Sixteen

The mystery of Jim was not only a topic which enjoyed a fair measure of flexibility; it was also a subject which many a theorist have found hard to put aside. From the time he went astray, more than a dozen theories have been advanced to best explain his eclipse. To date, none has been particularly convincing. Why is that so?

Firstly, what were Jim's motives for going over to the hill station? Moreover, what did he have in mind on completion of his stay at the area? According to Constance, "...he was a tired man... That was why he came here for a holiday." She was also quoted in the press as saying "he was looking forward to going back to Bangkok." But was this his actual arrangement? Not so. What Constance was trying to put across was that Jim had in fact made plans with her and the Lings to head for Singapore on the morning of March 27. The Lings were to drive him to the city state so that he would be able to keep his dinner appointment with Francis Joseph Galbraith, the US ambassador to Singapore and Edward Pollitz, an American capitalist who was exploring the possibility of establishing a textile outfit in the republic. But a day earlier, he went missing. How did this come about? Could it be that he got involved in a 'planned disappearance' or was it an 'unforeseen circumstance'? Based on circumstantial evidence, the former seems to be the case.

Prior to his leaving the country, Jim did get enmeshed with some "discoveries" which later resulted in him feeling sorry for himself. In 1962, for instance, he got into a misunderstanding with the Fine Arts Department (FAD) over his ownership of five statue heads. According to him, the items were purchased from an antiques dealer. He saw no harm in his having them. But the FAD felt otherwise. They were concerned of the growing rumors that the images were actually stolen from a cave in Northern Thailand. He tried to assure them that this was not the case. But the FAD did not think so. Finally, to put things right, he wrote to the FAD to inform them that "his house and its contents will belong to the Siamese people since I have already willed it to them by way of the Siam Society." The Department's Director-General did not respond to his letter. This made him upset. Later, the police came to his home to conduct an inspection of the stone pieces. An order was issued for them to be turned in. Jim complied with the demand and the necessary arrangements were made for the statue heads to be sent to the National Museum.

While all this was happening, Jim began to have a low opinion of the Siam Society. He felt, as beneficiaries of his estate, they could have done much more to prevent the sculptures from being taken away. But what he failed to understand was this: the heads were actually *stolen* items. In essence, the FAD had a legal right over them.

To show his disgust, he began to say all sorts of things. He told the press "first they decorate me (with *The Exalted Order of the White Elephant*) and then they raid me."

His dealings with the FAD and the Siam Society left him with a deep scar. To express his unhappiness, he resigned from the society's council and later saw to it that his will was revoked. Three years later, he prepared a second will. This time round, he arranged for his property to be left to his brother's son. The signing of the will was witnessed by Charles Sheffield and two other employees of the Thai Silk Company.

For the next few years, he felt uneasy staying in Thailand. His poor relationship with the FAD began to take a toll on him. It made him worry about his future and the ultimate ownership of his artifacts.

His fears were not unfounded. While he was still in office, the FAD's Director-General did express his unease over Jim's repository of collectibles. On occasions, he was quoted in the press as saying that Jim was one of the leaders who was involved with the looting of the country's temples.

It was such remarks that made Jim want to leave the country. In 1965, he had the liberty to do so. While on a trip to America, he could have stayed on had he wanted to. But he never did. Had he done so, he would have been made out as either a quitter or worse, someone who was indeed engaged with the plundering of the country's treasures.

So what alternatives did he really have? Nothing much, except to wait for an opportunity to come his way.

The chance surfaced when the Lings invited Constance to stay with them at Moonlight. In return, she extended the invitation to Jim. Even though he was bogged down with his company's expansion, Jim did not turn down her request. He capitalized on the invitation to leave Thailand for good.

Chapter Seventeen

Jim's friendship with the Lings and Constance was one that went back a long way. He not only knew them well; he had also stayed with them at Moonlight on two occasions. While on vacation, he was in the habit of moving around alone. He was usually seen at the center's lake and forested areas.

The Highlands served as an ideal setting for his planned disappearance. It was not only one of Malaysia's most popular destinations; it was also a place with a rich history. When compared to the other places of interest, the haunt had a lot more to offer. It covered an oddball mix of wild animals, dense jungles, deep ravines, hard-core communists, serene lakes, meandering streams, places of worship, animal traps, soaring peaks, government rest houses, rolling greens, kidnappers, gangsters, hillocks, colonial mansions, bandits, reptiles, country-styled inns, nurseries, orchards, vegetable farms, rivers, tea plantations, waterfalls, quicksand, insect life, scenic spots, a wintry climate and last but not least, its awe-inspiring natives.

It could be taken that Jim's getaway was well-planned. After leaving Moonlight, he was reportedly seen by five witnesses. None of them was right in their description of him, save the cook from the Lutheran abode.

As for the rest, it was either they saw the wrong person or the timing of their sightings was not correct. Che Fatimah binte Mohamed Yeh, the cook from the mission home, remembered seeing him at about 4pm. The servant employed at the Overseas Mission Fellowship bungalow also noticed him at around the same time. But that is not all. There were two other ladies who also saw him at about 4pm. One said she saw him at a side road talking to two passers-by. The other stated she spotted him a stone's throw away with a camera slung over his shoulders.

The only male witness who had a glimpse of him was an employee of the former Eastern Hotel. He was sure he saw someone who resembled Jim heading in the direction of the track which led to the golf course. But his description of Jim was not as one would expect. As such, his evidence was not taken seriously.

Out of the five who supposedly saw him, only Fatimah came up with an accurate description of him. Based on her testimony, it was apparent Jim left the Ling's domain and made a right turn for the Lutheran abode. The distance between the two addresses is about 1,440 meters. It takes about 30 minutes to cover this route.

What was it that made him want to head in that direction? The only clue available was that on his last trip he was stung by hornets about a kilometer from Moonlight. He did inform Constance and his other friends he would like to visit this spot on his next trip. Whether he did so or not, no one really knew. But a few conclusions could be drawn as a result of his being seen at the Lutheran compound: one, he had to stroll past Sunlight villa which was, incidentally, about 50 meters from where he stayed; two, for the next 480 meters, he had to carry on with his walk in order to reach the precinct's junction; three, on reaching the intersection, he had to make a right turn to ensure his arrival at the Lutheran complex; four, while walking along Jalan Kamunting (Kamunting Road), he had to cross two driveways which led to the residences of A43 and A44; five, after clearing both stretches, he had to carry on with his walk for another 560 meters; finally, after he had done all this, he found himself at the road barrier which separated the street from the domicile.

While he was standing at the gateway, there were two alternatives opened to him: one, he could have gone past the metal work and continued on with his walk; or two, he could have made an about turn and returned to where he first came from. Of the two, he chose the former. His decision to visit the property was indicative he was not on the lookout for a hornet's nest; it goes to show he was hunting for someone with whom he had earlier made an appointment.

The cook who spotted him mentioned she "...saw him come up the road (in other words, the 230-meter driveway)... He stopped for a while *to take a look at the garden. While looking at the plants,* he did not speak to anyone. A short while later he left the premises..."

What was it that made him want to leave the place? While he was at the quarters, it became obvious to him he had reached a dead end. Moreover, the person (or persons) he was searching for was not there. That said, he had no choice but to make a U-turn.

His visit to the Lutheran home was not his first. According to Fatimah, Jim had been to the property on two occasions. She went on to say he did have a certain fondness for the place. During his visits, he would usually spend some time inspecting the garden. On both instances he stayed behind for lunch. He somehow liked her cooking. This time round, he seemed to be troubled by something. After inspecting the plants, he sat on a boulder to take a rest. A few minutes later, he left the place.

When he left the chalet, she saw him walked down the 230-metre driveway. Unlike today, a fair amount of the approach could be seen from afar.

When he was about to reach the barrier area, there was a white car parked at the side of the driveway. From the distance, she saw him talking to someone who was in the vehicle. She could not make out who the person was. After a short exchange of words, the driver drove off.

When he reached the barrier spot, there were five options opened to him: one, he could have stayed at the entryway for a while; two, walked down the track near the barrier support area; three, scaled the steep slope to his left; four, gone down any one of the ravines to his right; or five, carried on with his walk. Since age was not on his side, it could be taken he was either picked up at this point or he opted to carry on with his walk. If he had gone on with his walk, he would have not only reached the road divider; he would have also had the prerogative of making a left turn or a right turn. A left turn would have seen him back at Moonlight; a right turn would have led him on to the main road. Since he failed to return and he was also not seen by anyone, then, it could be taken, he chose to remain on Jalan Kamunting for as long as he wanted to.

But could such an assessment be classified as correct? Some may say 'yes' but then again there will be many others who would be more than prepared to say 'no'. But what Richard Noone had had to say not only made sense; it also portrayed the fact that Jim did remain on Jalan Kamunting for a questionable period of time.

"I am fully convinced," Richard declared, "that Jim isn't in the jungle."

What was it that made him come to such a conclusion? There was no doubt Richard spent about thirty-six hours in the woods looking for Jim. Apart from hunting for Jim, his other role was to find out if the natives had buried Jim on the quiet. While he was in the green quietude, he came into contact with a few aborigines. As a result of his conversing with them, he could tell they were in no way trying to hide anything from him. In fact, when his brother Pat Noone got lost in the forest in the 1940s, it was the aborigines who kept Richard informed of his brother's fate. It was not a pleasant story to hear but Richard had to accept it the way it was told to him.

Of all the people who were connected with the sleuthing work, it could be confirmed that Richard was the only person who was bold enough to proclaim that "Jim isn't in the jungle."

Since Jim did not go into the wasteland, where then did he go to? From about 1.45pm to around four, he was on one side of Jalan Kamunting. A little after four he was on the same road but, this time, he was walking in the opposite direction. What was his purpose for being on this road for such a long time?

Whatever it was, it had nothing to do with the hornets which stung him a few years ago. It certainly had a lot to do with his keeping of an appointment.

But what indications were there to highlight that this was so? According to Helen, Jim "appeared nervous (while they were at the picnic) ... and he seemed anxious to get back early." If that be so, then at what time did they all come home? Dr. Ling remembered their returning at about 2.30pm. He was later quoted in *The Straits Times* as saying he "... heard footsteps pass by my bedroom door about 3.30pm and presumed it was Mr. Thompson taking a stroll."

Helen, however, had something else to say: she informed the *Eastern Sun* that Jim told her and Constance "Good night, sweethearts" at 1.30pm. When asked why the "good night" bit during noon, Helen remarked "it has always been our practice despite the time of the day or night to say good night whenever we wanted to retire for the night or for a siesta." The report concluded, "With the wave of his hand, he was gone."

Chapter Eighteen

There was no doubt Jim planned his disappearance prior to his coming over to the Highlands. His exit would have worked in his favor had he not visited the Lutheran habitat. In other words, if the cook did not see him, no one would have ever known where he went to on the day he went astray. But his sighting at the quarters left many in suspicion as to why he chose to go that way. It took him more than two hours to get there. For a rambler like Jim, he would have easily reached the place in about 30 minutes. Why then was he on Jalan Kamunting for more than two hours? Could it be that he was waiting for someone? Or could it be something else?

To begin with, what was it that made him want to visit the complex? The road he was on had three areas where a vehicle could make a three-point turn. The first was at the street's junction; the second was at the Lutheran's barrier area; and the third was within the compound of the mission home.

Out of the three, only two were for public use. When compared to the junction, the other spot was actually a dead end.

While he was standing at the barrier area, it could have occurred to him there was a mix-up with regards to the actual pickup point. He felt that whosoever was assigned to meet him could have mistakenly breezed pass the metal work and waited for him at the chalet instead. After a long wait, he decided to check out the place to see if this was really the case. Had he not done so, no one would have ever known he was on Jalan Kamunting that afternoon.

The mistake he made was but one. But there were other errors which were also made along the way.

The first involved Dr. Ling's remark that they got back from their picnic at 2.30pm. An hour later, he said he heard footsteps pass by his bedroom door and he "presumed it was Mr. Thompson taking a stroll." Helen, on the other hand, informed the press that Jim told her and Constance "Good night, sweethearts" at 1.30pm.

The question is this: Why the vast difference in timing? Could it be that Dr. Ling was not aware that Jim left the premises at 1.30pm? Or could it be he had a reason for saying things differently?

Apart from whatever was said, the two ladies witnessed his leave-taking at 1.30pm. As for Dr. Ling, he could only *presume* that Jim left his home at 3.30pm.

What followed after this has been somewhat puzzling; Jim's actual time of departure has hardly been brought up. Could it be that it was intentionally downplayed? Or could it be that it was conveniently forgotten? Come to think of it, there must be a reason for it.

If 3.30pm was taken into consideration, their activities for the day would have fallen to plan. In other words, they would have got up at eight, had breakfast, got changed, attended the church services, picked up a copy of the newspapers, headed back to Moonlight, collected their picnic hamper, drove on to Gunung Brinchang, had a picnic and returned at 2.30pm.

If 1.30pm was factored in, it would have been obvious that one of their activities was not carried out as announced. So which item in their program was done away with? Did they go to church on Easter

Sunday? They did. The foursome was seen by the congregation when they attended the services at 10.30am.

Since they went to church, could it also be taken they went for their picnic? Not so. The church services ended at about noon. If they had drove home to collect their hamper they would have reached Moonlight at about 12.15pm. The travelling time from Moonlight to Gunung Brinchang was more than an hour. In short, there was no way they could have gone for their picnic as planned.

Chapter Nineteen

It is a fact that Jim left Moonlight at about 1.30pm. He reached the junction of Jalan Kamunting at around 1.45pm. After making a right turn, he spent more than two hours making his way to the Lutheran Mission bungalow. Why did he have to select this route when there were so many other avenues available to him? Simple. He felt comfortable with this street because it was a suitable spot for his final appearance at the resort. In all, there were three houses situated along this 680-meter boulevard. After the Lee villa (unit A44), hardly anyone makes use of the rest of the road save those who were on vacation at the Lutheran dominion. He was aware that by remaining on this 560-meter stretch of road, the odds of his being chanced upon were as good as zero.

When he visited the Lutheran lodge, it became apparent to him the people he was supposed to meet were not there. When he left the property, he came into contact with the driver of a white car. After a brief exchange of words, the driver drove off. The questions that came to mind were these: Who was the driver of the vehicle? Did he know Jim? Did he ask for directions? Was he assigned to relay a message to Jim? Did he threaten Jim? Was the vehicle a Malaysian registered car or was it one with a foreign license plate? Was the driver Dr. Ammundsen? Or was it Dr. Ling?

According to Fatimah, Jim did not board the vehicle. He simply went on with his walk. While he was on Jalan Kamunting, there were two things that could have happened: one, he could have been picked up; or two, nothing of that sort. Of the two, the former was more the case. On the day he went missing, two black cars were seen travelling along Jalan Besar in the direction of Tapah. Jim was seen in one of the cars when it passed the Cameron Highlands Golf Club. He was seen by the golfers who were at the 14th hole. The distance between the green and the main road is within view. Since there was nothing amiss, the golfers took things in their stride and went on with their game.

The black cars, both with Thai license plates, continued on with their journey to Tapah. These were the same limousines that were spotted at the town in the late morning. While the cars were travelling down Jalan Besar, did they stop at the 30th mile of Ringlet? No.

It has been said the two vehicles did stop at the Foster's Lakehouse in order for Jim to alight. It became the talk of the town that Jim was escorted by two Asians to a path at the rear of the motel. While walking the track, Jim was allegedly stabbed in the forehead. What followed from here was anyone's guess.

Contrary to popular belief, this report was incorrect. The two cars did not stop at Ringlet. After passing the 30th Mile of Ringlet, the cars were seen at Tapah. They were spotted by the same group of workers who saw them in the late morning. This time round Jim was seen in one of the vehicles. The workers did not pay much attention to Jim. They were carried away by the size and design of the two cars.

Chapter Twenty

The sighting of Jim at Tapah proved to be intriguing. The question that begged an answer was this: Who was behind Jim's eclipse from the hill station? Was it the CIA, the communists, the triads or Jim's enemies?

Out of the four, the triads are out. According to an ex-triad leader, "the underworld had nothing to do with Jim's disappearance." The tiger general went on to say if "the triads were engaged, a ransom would have followed."

If the triads were not involved, who then was accountable for Jim's exit? Could it be his enemies? Whoever they were, they were not to be ruled out altogether. Before Jim came to the outpost, there was talk that an ex-prisoner was out to kill him. It is said the former captive served a twenty-year jail term. He was released from detention towards the end of 1966.

In public, Jim had nothing much to say about the ex-detainee. In private, he considered this man to be a threat to his life.

Jim was indeed a troubled man. On the one hand, he had problems with the Thai authorities. On the other, he was shadowed by someone who was out to destroy him.

Did these issues have an effect on him? It did. As time slipped by, he preferred to be left alone. This tendency of wanting to be detached was shown on a few occasions.

The first was on Sunday, March 5, 1967, when he joined a team of explorers to inspect some caves in northern Thailand. Their mission was to photograph the walls and ceilings of the grottos.

When they got to their destination, the crew stopped for a while to take a break. After the interval, they drove to the caves. Since they had the whole day to themselves, they took their time to study the caves in detail. Just as their outing was about to end, Jim informed them he would meet them at their earlier start-off point.

When the party headed that way, Jim was not to be found. An hour later, he was spotted a few kilometers from where they were supposed to meet. Tired and thirsty, he had nothing to say.

His other displays of wanting to be alone were manifested three weeks later. Whilst on a tour of Penang, he became anxious to get a haircut. Constance was uptight with his request. On their way back, she saw to it that he was dropped off at a barbershop.

Two days later, his longing for some solitude surfaced again. While the Lings and Constance were preparing themselves for church, Jim informed them he would meet them at the main road. While walking down Jalan Strawberry Park, he was all by himself. Later he met them at Jalan Besar and they all drove on to All Souls' Church.

Why was he behaving like this? Could it be that he was unhappy with his life? Or could it be something else?

Before he came to the resort, there was a brief mention in the *Bangkok World* that he would be taking a short holiday.

When he came to the tourist center, his first day at Moonlight was uneventful. The next morning, Dr. Ling and he got lost while exploring the woods.

After lunch, he withdrew for an afternoon siesta. At about 4.30pm he got up for some tea. Later, his companions and he joined Dr. Ammundsen at Ye Olde Smokehouse for dinner. After supper, they decided to call it a day.

While having dinner with Dr. Ammundsen, did the Dane tell him something?

Chapter Twenty-One

Jim's outing at the enclave was not so much of a holiday; it was actually one with a hidden agenda.

At the outset, his travel arrangements were different from previous trips. In the past, Helen would contact her rental agent to keep him informed of Jim's arrival date and time. On his part, he would notify taxi driver Liew Ah Tong to meet Jim and Constance at Malaysia's Subang airport. Ah Tong would then drive the two of them from Kuala Lumpur to Moonlight. This time round, the itinerary was different: Jim and Constance spent a day in Penang. When they got to Tapah, Ah Tong was not there to meet them. The rental agent was not instructed to arrange so.

At Tapah, Jim and Constance had to put up with a change of drivers and vehicles. This was necessary because the driver who had driven them from Penang was not feeling well when he got over to Tapah. When they were asked to board "Thompson's" taxi, there were two Chinese passengers in it. "Thompson" disclosed it was Constance who was against the idea of their having to share their ride with the other two commuters. After some deliberation, the local travelers were asked to get off and "Thompson" saw to it that Jim and Constance were driven on their own to Moonlight.

When Jim went astray, many things were written about him. In a report published in *The Straits Times* dated March 28, 1967, it was stated that "Yesterday at 3.30pm he (Jim) went out for a walk. When he failed to return at 8.30pm his friend (who asked that his name not be published) contacted the police." What could be made out of this? Was Dr. Ling a publicity-shy person? Or was there a reason for having his name omitted?

Diffidence aside, why did Dr. Ling and Helen agree to disagree on Jim's actual time of departure? Could it be that one was telling the truth; the other wasn't? A time difference of two hours was indeed significant. Many things could have happened within that period of time. There was no excuse Dr. Ling did not know that Jim left the premises at 1.30pm. It was much the same for those who wrote about him. Jim's time of leave-taking was widely covered in the morning edition of the *Eastern Sun*. Thousands read about it. Not to know of it is as good as being untruthful to oneself.

Further to this, there was a separate development which proved to be somewhat puzzling. Before he came to the haven, Jim made arrangements with Constance and the Lings to head for Singapore on the morning of March 27. Dr. Ling was to drive him to the city state so that he would be able to keep his dinner appointment with Francis Joseph Galbraith, the US ambassador to Singapore and Edward Pollitz, an American businessman who was exploring the possibility of setting up a textile outfit in the republic. But a day earlier, he disappeared. What caught many by surprise was this: his appointment was cancelled before he got lost. This prompted Constance to ask: "Why did the embassy cancel his dinner appointment *before* and not *after* he went missing?"

Chapter Twenty-Two

The mystery of Jim was not as complex as what one would have made it out to be. It was a far cry as compared to the disappearance of Judge Joseph Force Crater. Judge Crater vanished in New York on August 6, 1930. He was last seen leaving a restaurant on 45th Street. His exit became one of the most famous mysteries in American history. It earned him the title of "The Missingest Man in New York." The message, "Judge Crater, call your office" is still a popular line in America. So far, Judge Crater has not called. Neither has Jim.

In the case of Jim, there is sufficient proof he sneaked off for an anonymous existence. His trip to the refuge could be regarded as the watershed of his life. While he was at the haunt, there were many things that came into play. Most of it was planned before he came over to the Highlands.

On Easter Sunday, his friends and he did attend the morning services at All Souls' Church. But they did not picnic at Gunung Brinchang. To make it seem as though they went that way, Helen admitted that Jim "appeared nervous ... and he seemed anxious to get back early." It was also reported he "started collecting the plates" before the outing ended. Since they did not go to the picnic, then, whatever was said about him was not true. But, debunkers may argue, a photograph of him was taken while he was at the picnic. Yes, a snapshot of him was taken. It was even featured in a number of publications. But was the photograph taken at Gunung Brinchang? No. It was either taken at Moonlight or elsewhere. There are two reasons for this: firstly, the slope gradient of the site was a lot gentler when compared to the one depicted in the photograph. Secondly, back in the 1960s, no one went that way for an outdoor meal. Why? The place was terrorized by the communists. If the foursome had gone there as what they claimed, chances were they had a picnic with the communists. It was only in the 1970s that things changed. When it was evident the communists were no longer a threat, many headed for the summit to picnic near the fenced area of the radio and television station.

Next, when Jim walked out of Moonlight, it was reported he left his suit jacket, a pill box, a packet of cigarettes and a lighter behind. Yes, he did leave his suit jacket behind. But it was unlikely he forgot to bring along his pill box, lighter and cigarettes. Why was that so? In the first place, he did not creep out of the estate. He left the house with the full knowledge of Helen and Constance. If he had forgotten his cigarettes, they would have reminded him about it. If they did not to do so, he would have returned to get them. Any chain smoker would have done that. If this line of thinking seemed unacceptable, then consider this: While he was approaching the barrier area of Moonlight, Mohamad, the gardener, saw him light up a cigarette. Where then did the lighter and cigarette come from?

Regardless of the cigarettes, the one point which was seldom discussed was Jim's behavior when he had his last meal at Moonlight. After lunch, he had a beer. But Jim was unlike the rest. He did not finish his beer. After consuming half of it, he got up and walked to the veranda. Helen and Constance came after him. It was here that they had a short conversation. Later, he waved goodbye to the two of them and left the scene.

Why didn't he finish his beer? Could it be that he did not like their company? Or could it be that he had to meet up with someone? Of the two, the latter comes closer to the truth.

On the day he disappeared, Jim was seen in one of the two black cars when it got over to Tapah. He was not blind-folded. There was no handkerchief tied to his mouth. He did not put on a hat. He did not have on a pair of sunglasses. He did not put up any resistance. He did not shout for help. In short, he was both cool and collected.

Where then did the two vehicles head to? To Lumut? To Sadao? Or to Padang Besar? Contrary to popular belief, they did not head to any of the assumed destinations. The two cars were seen heading in the direction of Subang.

What happened after this? Did Jim leave the country? He did. Two months after he was declared as lost, he was seen in Tahiti. According to Edward Pollitz, he was sure he saw Jim leaving a hotel while he was on a trip to the island. He recalled his attempt of going after Jim just as he was about to leave the premises. But before he could do so, Jim got into a waiting car and left the scene.

There are several questions that come to mind. Firstly, was Edward telling the truth? Secondly, why was Jim in Tahiti? Finally, was he there on transit?

When Jim left the mansion he had no passport on him. His passport was with Constance. She showed it to the police when they came over to Moonlight. If he did not have a passport, how then did he leave the country?

What is puzzling is that Jim's relocation to Tahiti was hardly brought up. If so, it was briefly touched on.

While travelling with Jim in "Thompson's" taxi, Constance recalled that "Jim was not his usual self." She added, "He was in an awful frame of mind. I could tell something was up."

But "Thompson" took Jim to be otherwise. He considered Jim to be a nice man. As for Constance, he made her out to be both stern and talkative.

Constance certainly had a lot more to say when compared to Jim. Apart from nagging about their incident at Tapah, she also tried to enquire about his future. But Jim cut her short. This was not the first time she brought up the subject. While they were touring Penang, she also mentioned about it. When Tahiti was broached, the taxi driver took it they were heading that way for a holiday.

What does this go to show? Isn't it indicative she had an idea as to where he was headed to?

Whatever has been said, Jim had "to pull a Crater." When he left Thailand, he spent a day in Penang. The next day, he was at the Highlands. Two days later, he left for Tahiti. Why Tahiti of all places?

Tahiti is the largest island in the Windward group of French Polynesia. When Jim was reportedly seen on the island, it had a population of about 70,000 inhabitants. Apart from Tahitian, French is the territory's official language.

Why then did Jim choose to go there? Wouldn't he have problems communicating with the islanders? Not so.

During the Second World War, Jim served as a commissioned officer in the Office of Strategic Services – the frontrunner to the Central Intelligence Agency. His first call of duty was with the French resistance forces in North Africa. Later, arrangements were made for him to be sent to Europe. At the height of the Second World War, large areas of the Continent were under the control of the Germans. Jim was sent to Europe because he communicated well in French. While engaged in France, he capitalized on his fluent French to gain an advantage over the enemy. When the war in Europe ended on May 8, 1945, he was transferred to Ceylon.

As far as Jim was concerned, communicating in French was not a problem. When he had to deal with the Indo-Chinese, he did not communicate with them in their mother tongue. He spoke to them in French.

If he reportedly found his way to Tahiti, then it is not necessary to get involved in a guessing game as to who picked him up and where exactly he was dropped off. Come to think of it, all this was planned long before he came over to the Highlands.

Postscript

To date, volumes have been written about Jim Thompson, by far, the best known legend of Southeast Asia. Of the many who wrote about him, none have come close to solving his disappearance from the resort. Why is that so? There are two reasons for this: one, it could be the authors were not aware that Jim actually left the Ling's estate at 1.30pm; or two, they chose not to know about it. Of the two, the latter seems to be more the case. As such, his sudden eclipse has not only gone on to become an unsolved mystery; it has also led many to go on a tangent.

I first came to have an interest in Jim's exit as a result of reading about it in the newspapers. My initial impression was that he got lost as a consequence of falling into a pit of quicksand. Years later, I came to realize I was wrong.

In 1994, while on a trip to the retreat, it came as a surprise to me that in spite of the fact he vanished more than 25 years ago, the memory of his departure was still fresh in the minds of many. What also caught my attention was this: some of the residents I spoke to were sure he had a hidden motive for coming over to their neighborhood. But, due to a lack of evidence, they had to put away their views.

While I was at the hill station, I came to have an interest in his absconding all over again. To satisfy my curiosity, I took the route which he took just after he left Moonlight. While walking down Jalan Kamunting, several questions crossed my mind: One, why did he have to choose this route when there were so many other avenues opened to him? Two, was he really on the lookout for a hornet's nest? Three, what were his intentions for heading for the Lutheran Mission bungalow? Four, was he aware a mission home existed at the end of the road? Five, while he was at the complex, what made him want to leave the place? Six, on his return, did he scale the steep slope to his left? Lastly, did he have an appointment to be picked up by someone with whom he had earlier made arrangements with?

After giving it serious thought, it dawned on me there was more to it than his being on the hunt for a hornet's nest. When I got back from the outpost, I went through a stack of files to see if I could pinpoint the exact time he left the villa. To the best of my knowledge, I remembered being told he departed the scene at about 1.30pm. What later proved to be a disappointment was that most reports, if not all, claimed he walked out of Moonlight at 3.30pm. Much later, while going through the past issues of the *Eastern Sun*, I came across an article which not only stated he left the premises at 1.30pm; equally interesting, it also affirmed that Jim waved goodbye to Helen and Constance prior to his leaving the compound. Armed with this detail and other facts as well, I went ahead to write a book entitled: *SOLVED! The Mysterious Disappearance of Jim Thompson, the Legendary Thai Silk King*. It was printed and published in the United Kingdom in 1996. Eight years later, my work was also published in America. Of the many who read my book, none came around to say they were "short changed."

I have to admit it was not easy solving Jim's exit from the Cameron Highlands. Over the years, a lot has been written about him. But what has been written about him did not bring his departure to a satisfying close. At best, it was an unsolved mystery; at worse, it was a rehash of what others had had to say. For starters, most writers did not visit the Highlands. Not surprisingly, many did not come up with a sketched map of the resort. For the few who did so, the Lutheran home was somehow left out. Could it be an oversight? Not so. An attempt to mislead comes closer. If the unit had been included, the reader would have sensed something was amiss. To prevent that from happening, the authors did away with the location of the house.

Writing about Jim Thompson was no easy task. It involved reading up on him, talking to the right people, trekking the jungle and last but not least, staying at Moonlight. When compared to the others, I have to admit I was in a better position. I am a Singaporean. I communicate well in English, Malay and a Chinese dialect. I am at home when I am in Malaysia. I love their food. I am aware of their customs and traditions. I have worked in Malaysia, Brunei and Indonesia. Yes, I was educated in Singapore but what matters most is I know when to talk and when to keep quiet.

For this edition, I visited the haven again in October 2009. While I was at the enclave, I took the opportunity to visit Gunung Brinchang. It took me and a Malaysian friend about an hour to reach the mountain top. While we were at the summit, we spent some time examining the picnic site where a snapshot of Jim was taken in the past. Surprising as it may seem, the photograph was not as one would expect. The site's slope gradient was a lot different when compared to that of the photograph. Further, the angle that the shot was taken was indicative that the shot was taken somewhere else.

Apart from visiting Gunung Brinchang, I also spent a day at the Jalan Kamunting precinct. I enjoyed my stroll from Moonlight to the Lutheran abode: it not only gave me a nice "feel" of the route which Jim took; it also made me more aware as to why he opted for this path. Except for the presence of a government-owned building (*Rumah Istirahat*

Kumpulan Wang Simpanan Perkerja), nothing much has changed in the area since the time Jim went astray. Throughout my walk, I hardly came into contact with anyone. It was much the same when I traveled this road some years back.

If you are planning a trip to the hamlet, this is the one place you should not miss. Only after you have visited this place would you be in a better position to understand why Jim was on this street for more than two hours and on it again for a questionable period of time.

Epilogue

Brigadier-General Edwin Black got to know Jim in the 1940s. It was he who persuaded Jim to join the Office of Strategic Services (OSS) – the frontrunner of the Central Intelligence Agency.

General Black was born in New Orleans, Louisiana, USA, on August 17, 1915. In 1940, he was commissioned as a Second Lieutenant after graduating from the US Military Academy at West Point, New York.

From 1943 to 1945, he served as a member of the OSS in England, France and Germany. He was instrumental in having Jim transferred to the OSS during this period of time.

After the Second World War, he took up several postings in the United States, Europe and Southeast Asia.

His first tour of duty to the Far East was in 1958. After a short stint, he returned to the United States. In 1964, he was sent to Vietnam. Two years later, he became the commander of the U.S. Army Support Forces based at Camp Friendship, Korat, Thailand.

During his military career, he was awarded the Bronze Star Medal, the Joint Service Commendation Medal (with one Oak Leaf Cluster) and the Senior Parachutist's Badge.

After leaving the army, General Black retired in Honolulu, Hawaii. He died of a cardiac arrest in 1985. He was 69.

Charles U. Sheffield, who took over Jim as Managing Director of the Thai Silk Company, died of cancer in 1973. While he was alive, the Texan was steadfast in his view that Jim met his fate as a result of an accident in the jungle.

Che Fatimah binte Mohamed Yeh, the cook who saw Jim when he strolled into the grounds of the Lutheran dominion, passed away on July 4, 2009.

She was one of the five witnesses who came forward to keep the police informed after Jim was proclaimed as missing. Unlike the others, her testimony was the most credible.

She was in the kitchen when Jim came over to the cottage. After inspecting the garden, she saw him walk down the driveway. When he was about to reach the barrier area, she saw him stop to talk to someone in a white car. From the distance, she could not make out who the person was. After a short exchange of words, the car left the scene.

The police found her revelation to be particularly useful. It did help them to be more focused in their hunt for Jim.

After Jim vanished from the retreat, Fatimah continued to work at the mission home for some time. Later, she was employed as a cook at one of the chalets owned by the late cinema magnate Loke Wan Tho.

Before she died, she was hospitalized for being down with pneumonia. She passed away at the age of 66, leaving behind a husband and two daughters.

Chin Peng, a long-time leader of the outlawed Malayan Communist Party (MCP), was suspected by the press for having a hand in Jim's exit from the resort.

Chin Peng was born Ong Boon Hua on October 22, 1924 in Perak, West Malaysia. In 1940, he was accepted as a probationary member of the MCP.

He rose to prominence during the Japanese Occupation (1942-1945) when many Malaysian Chinese took to the woods to fight against the Japanese. These fighters became known as the Malayan People's Anti-Japanese Army (MPAJA). Chin Peng served as liaison officer between the MPAJA and the British who were stationed in Southeast Asia.

After the war, Chin Peng was elected as the Secretary General of the MCP. An anti-colonialist, he was notorious for leading the party's insurgency during the Malayan Emergency.

In 1948, a State of Emergency was declared by the colonial government when the members of the MCP killed three Europeans at Sungei Siput, Perak. The hostilities went on for 12 years. When it came to an end in 1960, Chin Peng left the country. The MCP withdrew to the Malaysian-Thai border and regrouped as the Communist Party of Malaya (CPM). They continued with their ideological struggle for the next two decades.

The CPM finally laid down its arms in 1989. That same year, separate agreements were signed involving the CPM and the governments of Malaysia and Thailand. Since then, he has gone on to live in exile.

Constance (Connie) Mangskau was born in Chiang Mai, Thailand in 1907 to an English father and Thai mother. She was educated in Thailand and later in Singapore where she became a nurse. At 18, she married a Norwegian rubber planter. She was widowed at a young age.

During the Japanese Occupation, Constance was imprisoned in Cambodia for being a spy. After the war, she got to know Jim while she was engaged as an interpreter for the Allied Services based in Bangkok. Later, she made a career switch to the retailing of antiques. Jim helped her set up Monogram Antiques at the Trocadero Hotel in 1951. With time, her venture into antiques proved to be a success. Before she died in 1990, she was acknowledged as being one of Bangkok's leading dealers in the decorative arts and craft of Southeast Asia.

Dean F. Frasche got to know Jim in the 1960s. It was he who encouraged Jim to turn to ceramics after Jim got into a row with Thailand's Fine Arts Department.

Dean spent much of his working life in the Far East. He passed away on August 23, 1994 at the age of 88.

His interests in ceramics started in the 1930s while he was employed as a surveyor for the Belgian government in the Philippines. He was exposed to Asian ceramics in 1937 when he was brought to a cave on the island of Minalog in the Philippines. The cavern he visited was filled with shards of Ming dynasty blue-and-white porcelain. From that moment, his interest in earthenware became a permanent and consuming part of his life.

After the Second World War, he became the Vice-President of Union Carbide's mining operations in Thailand.

In 1976, he organized the first exhibition of Southeast Asian ceramics in America at the Asia Society based in Manhattan, New York City. He was the author of the exhibition's catalogue entitled *Southeast Asian Ceramics: Ninth through Seventeenth Century.*

Dean was into ceramics for almost forty years of his life. He was not only a respected authority on the subject of china; he was also someone who helped introduce a new perspective to this field of study.

Dr. Dadi Balsara drew out Jim's 'astrological chart' to see if the 'stars' could provide him with a clue as to where Jim could be found. Later, it became evident his findings were really of not much of a help.

Dr. Balsara was responsible for setting up Perfumes of Singapore (Private) Ltd on June 10, 1969. The principal activities of the company involved the manufacture of perfumes, fragrances and essential oils. He became the company's Managing Director on November 16, 1973. In 1989, he founded Mount Everest Mineral Water Limited. Situated at Dhaula Kuan in Himachal Pradesh, India, the company is one of the largest mineral water plants in Asia. He resigned as the company's Chairman and Managing Director on September 26, 2003. His wife, Mrs. Christina Balsara, a non-Executive Director, resigned on October 1, 2003.

Born in Mumbai, India, Dr. Balsara holds a master's degree in chemistry and a doctorate in homeopathic medicine. After earning a Ph. D in psychiatry, he went into private practice.

In the 1960s, he married Christina Lee, the divorced wife of cinema magnate Loke Wan Tho. The ex-beauty queen was appointed a Director of Perfumes of Singapore (Private) Ltd on November 9, 1969.

Over the years, the company has produced a wide variety of fragrances; its renowned brands were 'Singapore Girl' and 'Bali'. The company ceased to exist on February 1, 2008.

Dr. Einar Ammundsen was introduced to Jim in the late 1940s. He was at the Cameron Highlands when Jim disappeared from the haven.

Dr. Ammundsen passed away on March 7, 1999. He married Aks (Ullitz?), his teenage girlfriend in 1979. Both Aks and he were previously married but their spouses died before them.

He left Denmark for Thailand after the Second World War. While residing in Thailand, he and Aks became well known figures among the members of the Scandinavian community.

In 1995, Dr. Ammundsen retired from his medical practice. That same year, he and Aks returned to Denmark. Aks passed away on June 21, 2009.

Dr. Ling Tien Gi was sixty-nine years old when Jim vanished from the old British station. Twenty-five years later, he died while he was on a short stay in the United States. His obituary, which was inserted by Dr. Tan Eng Liang, F.E. Zuellig (Singapore) Pte Ltd, Hugo Arnet and Pierre Moccand, in *The Straits Times* on March 14, 1992, was penned as follows:

> *Dr T.G. Ling, recipient of the Singapore Science Council's first gold medal, died on March 9, 1992, in Seattle, USA after a brief illness. He was 94.*
>
> *Dr Ling, a native of Swatow, China, graduated from Shanghai Baptist College (later the University of Shanghai) in 1919 with a degree in chemistry. Two years later he won a competitive scholarship from the American Baptist Mission and went to the USA for post-graduate studies. There he received a master's degree from Brown University in 1922 and a Ph.D. in industrial chemistry from Cornell University in 1924.*
>
> *In 1926 he returned to China where he developed the first matches that would light during the rainy season in the Yangtze River Valley. Later he was responsible for setting government standards and testing procedures for vegetable oils. For a time he headed the government's inspection and certification laboratory for vegetable oils in Wuhan. There he established a reputation for sincerity and honesty in an area of commerce that had been marked by bribery and corruption.*
>
> *During World War II he managed the Chinese government's monopoly of materials for making matches. Through his efforts the Chinese match industry became totally self-sufficient, utilizing locally available resources to substitute for imported chemicals which had been cut off by the Japanese occupation.*
>
> *In 1951 he moved to Singapore where he became affiliated with the Zuellig Company in establishing the first factory (Gold Coin Ltd) for manufacturing scientifically balanced poultry and pig feeds. His introduction of these feeds along with improved breeds and methods of raising poultry and pigs greatly improved the efficiency of producing animal protein in Singapore and elsewhere in Southeast Asia. It also gave rise to a multi-million dollar animal feed industry. The high quality and low price of chicken and pork in Singapore today are the results of his efforts. His*

contribution was recognized by the Singapore Science Council which awarded him its first gold medal in 1969. The medal was presented by (then) Prime Minister Lee Kuan Yew in a formal ceremony.

Following his success in Singapore and Malaysia, Dr Ling was sought after as a consultant in other countries. He traveled to Indonesia, Thailand, Tonga and Vietnam to give advice on improving their animal feed industries. He was awarded the insignia of the Fifth Class (member) of the Most Noble Order of the Crown of Thailand for his contribution there.

He was formerly the Managing Director of Singapore Agri-Enterprises Pte Ltd, Chairman of the Board of Directors of Island Livestock Pte Ltd, and member of the Boards of Directors of Gold Coin Ltd, National Grain Elevator Ltd and Primary Enterprises Ltd, Singapore. After (his) retirement in 1990 he moved to Seattle.

Dr Ling and his late wife, Helen, were well known socially, particularly in the Singapore American community. She died in 1982. They were featured in the news in 1967 when Jim Thompson, known as the Thai silk king, disappeared from their bungalow in Cameron Highlands, Malaysia. That mystery has never been solved.

He is survived by two brothers, Myron Ling of Mitcham, South Australia and Theodore Ling of Scottsdale, Arizona; one son, Colonel James Ling, US Air Force (retired) of Arlington, Virginia; and three grandchildren.

Edward Pollitz, the American businessman who was supposed to meet up with Jim in Singapore, is the only person who saw Jim after he vanished from the Cameron Highlands. He saw Jim leaving a hotel in Tahiti about two months after he was declared as lost. He recalled his attempt of going after him just as he was about to leave the hotel's premises. But, before he could do so, Jim quickly got into a waiting car and left the scene. Six months later, Edward was asked whether the person he saw was indeed Jim. He was positive it was Jim. He went on to say that when Jim got into the car there was an elderly lady seated at the rear of the vehicle. He tried to trace the man he saw but his search drew a blank.

Edward was into textiles for many years of his life. In the mid-1960s, he was called upon to serve as an adviser to the Singapore International Executive Service and the now-defunct Singapore Economic Development Organization. He served both establishments for less than three years. He died of leukemia in August, 1968. He was 68 years old.

George Barrie, Jim's friend and co-founder of the Thai Silk Company, died in Bangkok of a heart attack on May 2, 1996. He lived to the age of 94.

Helen Ling (nee Dalling), was born in Ohio, USA, in 1901. She was a renowned dealer and connoisseur of Chinese art.

In 1928, she married Dr. Ling Tien Gi, a Chinese chemist. They lived in China, Hong Kong and Singapore. She ran a few antique shops in Shanghai from 1938 to 1949. When the communists came to power, her husband and she left China for Hong Kong. In 1951, they moved to Singapore. While residing in Singapore, she developed an interest for Southeast Asian antiquities. In 1969, she became one of the founding members of the Southeast Asian Ceramic Society whose first president was William Willetts.

Apart from chinaware, Helen also had a penchant for Thai silk. She got to know Jim Thompson in the 1950s. She was the first person to promote his silk products in Singapore.

In the 1960s, she had three shops which sold antiques, paintings, furniture, ceramics, silk and jade. Her shops were located on Tanglin Road, the former Hotel Singapura Inter-Continental and the Cathay Hotel Shopping Arcade (now the Cathay Building).

In the mid-1970s, two of her shops had to make way for urban development in the area. Towards the end of the 1970s, her flagship shop at 101 Tanglin Road began to run out of space. In 1980, she moved her business to Park House, 21 Orchard Boulevard.

Since coming to Singapore, Helen was active in the promotion of Chinese art. Her shop – Helen D. Ling – was a landmark of Tanglin as what China Art House was to Orchard Road. Before she died on May 15, 1982, she was one of the four shareholders of her company. The others were Dr. Ling Tien Gi, Carole Y. Wong and John Wong Cheung Ching.

Lieutenant Denis Horgan, the aide to Brigadier-General Black, became the editor of the English-language *Bangkok World* after he left the army. Later, he worked for the *Boston Globe,* the *Washington Star* and the *Hartford Courant.* His job as a journalist took him to many places. Most people are familiar with his work for the *Hartford Courant.* His contributions to this publication won him a number of national awards.

Michael Ian Vermont was told of Jim's sighting at Tapah a few days after Jim went missing. He tried to deceive Dr. Ling into believing that Jim was kept in a house. His attempt to mislead Dr. Ling proved to be a flop.

Michael, an Indonesian of Javanese descent, left Singapore in 1982 for reasons that were best known to himself. Prior to his departure, he was involved with a number of "investment schemes" which were more a figment of his imagination than anything else.

Peter Hurkos died in Los Angeles, California on June 1, 1988. Website *http://www.stephanyhurkos.com/peter.htm* dated September 11, 2009 had this to say about him:

Peter Hurkos is considered by experts to have been the world's foremost psychic. Born May 21, 1911, in Dordrecht, Holland, he acquired his psychic gift in 1941 after falling from a ladder and suffering a brain injury. He was in a coma for three days at the Zuidwal Hospital. Upon regaining consciousness, he discovered he had developed an ability to pierce the barriers that separate the past, present and future. With stunning accuracy, he was able to see into the unknown.

Hurkos gained worldwide acceptance as a psychic detective, working on cases involving missing planes, persons, and murder victims after his fall. Some of his most illustrious cases were "The Stone of Scone" [London, England], "The Boston Strangler Multiple Murders" [Boston, Massachusetts], "The Missing Thai Silk King, Jim Thompson" [Asia/Thailand], "The Ann Arbor Co-Ed Murders" [Ann Arbor, Michigan], and "The Sharon Tate Murders" [Los Angeles, California].

In 1956, Hurkos was brought to the United States by Andrija Puharich, MD (died 1994) to be tested at his Glen Cove, Maine medical research laboratory. For two-and-a-half years he was tested under tightly controlled conditions. The results convinced Dr. Puharich that Hurkos' psychic abilities were far greater than any he had ever tested (before or thereafter)... a remarkable 90% accuracy.

Hurkos' forte was psychometry, the ability to see past-present-future associa-tion by touching objects... He had been a consultant to every President of the United States from Eisenhower to Reagan. Hurkos received countless police badges from police chiefs around the world, including one from the International Police Association, and INTERPOL. His Holiness, Pope Pius XII, decorated Hurkos stating: "I hope you will always use your God-given gift for the betterment of mankind. Use it as an instrument to touch the people, to help them."

Pridi Panomyong a.k.a. Luang Pradist Manudharm died in France on May 2, 1983. Born on May 11, 1900, he became Thailand's first popularly elected Prime Minister in 1946. A year later, he fled the country when he was suspected for having a hand in the assassination of King Ananda.

It is said, he secretly returned to Thailand in 1949 to stage a *coup d'état* against the dictatorship of Luang Pibulsongram. When it failed, he left the country for China. From China, he moved to France, where he spent the rest of his life.

Many who were close to him were positive he had nothing to do with Jim's vanishing from the Cameron Highlands.

Richard Noone, a Cambridge-trained anthropologist, first came to Malaya (now Malaysia) in 1939. When the Japanese swept down the Malay Peninsula in 1941, Richard and his brother, H.D. (Pat)

Noone were forced to go their separate ways: Pat, an anthropologist with the State of Perak, chose to retire to the woods; Richard headed for Australia where he served as an Intelligence Officer with the "Z" Experimental Station (ZES) in Cairns, Queensland. ZES – a branch of the Inter-Allied Services Department – was formed to conduct sporadic raids on the Japanese.

After the war, Richard worked for the Australian Intelligence Service before moving back to Malaya in 1950. Three years later, General Sir Gerald Templer, the ex-British High Commissioner to Malaya appointed him as head of the Malayan Department of Aborigines (MDA).

Richard was responsible for the setting up of the Senoi Praaq, which is now part of the Royal Malaysian Police Force. It is made up of non-Malay tribal people known collectively as Orang Asli (aborigines). He pressed for its formation to stop the communist influence over the aboriginal settlements in the deep jungles of the country. In 1956 General Templer agreed to the inclusion of the Senoi Praaq as an arm of the MDA. Noone served as the unit's commanding officer from 1957 to 1961. During his term of office, he and the Senoi Praaq were highly successful in diminishing the communist threat during the Malayan Emergency. The Emergency, which lasted for 12 years, ended in 1960.

In the course of his duties, Richard became aware that one of the peninsula's indigenous clans had a close link with the Montagnards that lived in Vietnam. In the 1960s, he led a group of Malayo-Polynesian tribesmen to the Central Highlands to work with them. The two groups had no difficulties getting along well. But the communists became suspicious of their growing "closeness." This led the Viet Cong to attach a unit to Richard's team. Over time, animosity developed between the Vietnamese and Richard's men. After a while, Richard and his team left the country. On his return from Vietnam, Richard took up a posting with the Southeast Asia Treaty Organization. He died of cancer in 1973 in Bangkok, Thailand.

Seni Pramoj, the former Prime Minister of Thailand passed away on July 6, 1997. He died of a chronic pulmonary disorder at the age of 92. Born into a minor branch of the royal family, Seni studied to be a lawyer and later ended up as the leader of the *Seri Thai* or Free Thai Movement. When the Japanese Occupation came to an end, he served as Premier for a short spell in an interim government which was formed in 1946. Thirty years later, he made a political comeback and was elected as the country's Prime Minister in 1975 and 1976. He left office in 1975 as a result of an electoral defeat. A year later, his government collapsed in a bloodless coup which was staged by the military.

"Thompson", the taxi driver who fetched Jim and Constance from Tapah to Moonlight, has not only mellowed with age; equally intriguing, he has also accepted the nickname "Thompson" despite the fact he has a given Chinese name. Of late, many things have been said about him, some true, some false. For instance, just after it became known that Jim was missing, there was talk that Jim hired his taxi and instructed him to stop and wait for him near the junction of Jalan Kamunting. This account is not true. According to "Thompson", Jim never made use of his services while he was residing at Moonlight. What actually transpired was this: when it became clear that Jim was not to be found, "Thompson" and two others decided to go into the woods to look for Jim. While doing so, they got lost along the way. Much later, his family members were informed his unattended vehicle was spotted near the junction of Jalan Kamunting. Sensing that something was not right, they engaged the services of a few aborigines to go out and find for him. A week later, all three were discovered in the jungles of Gopeng. After this episode, he became known as "Thompson".

Glossary

All Souls' Church: Located at Lot 68, Jalan Pejabat Hutan, the resort's little Church of England was once known to the early members of its congregation as The Cameron Highlands Church. The history of this establishment can be traced back to the 1950s when the Vicar of Ipoh and the other members of the expatriate clergy held their services at either the Cameron Highlands Hotel (now the Merlin Hotel) or the Slim School (which is presently the home of the Malaysian Commando Unit). In 1958, the church was extended an offer for a piece of land which used to adjoin the grounds of the former Slim School. The land, which was once owned by Miss Anne L.P. Griffith-Jones, was transferred to the Diocese on the understanding that a church would be built on it. To get things going, the members of the British army contributed a sum of US$1,220. Further to this, they also gave the church a dismantled "Nissen Hut". It has since served as the building's roof structure. The construction of the church was completed in 1958. The name "All Souls' Church" was given during its consecration ceremony which was held on April 30, 1959. The sanctification service was conducted by the Right Reverend Bishop H.W. Baines. Except for the addition of modern conveniences, the church has remained unchanged to this day.

Bencharong (*ben-cha-wrong*): A Thai five-colored chinaware which is noted the world over for its unique form, design and beauty. During the production process, only the finest clay is used to produce the ceramic. The popular combinations of colors are usually that of red, yellow, black, white and green.

Bukit (*boo-kit*): A Malay word meaning 'hill'.

Bomoh (*bow-more*): A Malay word meaning 'medium' or 'witch doctor'.

Communist Party of Malaya: Refer to **Chin Peng** in Epilogue section.

Foster's Lakehouse: Now known as The Lakehouse, this place once belonged to the late Colonel Stanley Foster. The Colonel is best remembered for the construction of the building which is situated at the 30th Mile of Ringlet. Colonel Forster died in 1984 and the Lakehouse has since come under the management of the Concorde group of hotels. In the past, a track near the inn was used by the communists to carry their clandestine activities at night. If you are thinking of exploring this route, be careful. The area was once covered with barbed wire.

Golden Triangle: A fairly large area in Asia where the common species of poppy (*papaver somniferum*) grows in abundance. This region, which borders four countries, namely, Laos, Burma (Myanmar), Thailand and China has been a hotbed of turmoil and conflict for a number of years. Most of the world's opium, the extract from which heroin is derived, comes from this district. Several attempts have been made in the past to discourage the hill tribes from cultivating this crop. But its cultivation is unlikely to be curtailed because the returns from this crop are far greater than what the other cash crops can offer.

Gunung (*goo'-nong*): A Malay word meaning 'mountain'.

Gurkha (*ger'-ker/goor'-car*): A military race who settled in the province of Gurkha, Nepal around the eighteenth century; a member of one of the famed Gurkha regiments of the British Army.

Iban (*e-ban*): An East Malaysian aborigine who is more often than not a resident of Sarawak.

Jalan (*jar-lan*): A Malay word meaning 'road'.

Jim Thompson's 'grave': A 47 km cycling loop covering the hamlet's Bertam Valley and Boh Tea plantations. The route can be taxing at some points. It is best to take your time and complete the circuit within a period of eight hours. For more details concerning the course, please visit *http://www.bikebash.freeservers.com/index.html.*

Jim Thompson's House: The mansion was constructed in 1959 when most expatriates preferred to stay in western-styles homes. During the construction stage, not a single nail was used. After the structure was built, it became a trend to construct homes that were patterned after his. The mansion which is situated opposite the National Stadium is worth a visit. It contains a wide assortment of artifacts. The house could be reached by public or private transport. Except for Sundays, it is open to the public from 9am to 4.30pm. Photography is not allowed within the abode. Admission is 100 bahts for adults and 50 bahts for those who are below the age of 25. Guides are available on request.

Klong (*ker-long*): A Thai word meaning 'canal' or 'waterway'.

Kramat hidup (*kra-mud he-dope*): A medium with supernatural powers.

Lumut: A small town in Perak, West Malaysia. It is the gateway to Pulau Pangkor (Pangkor Island) which is about 100km west of Ipoh, Perak.

The island covers an area of approximately eight square kilometers. It was once a favorite hideout for fishermen, sailors, merchants and pirates.

Lutheran Mission bungalow: Tucked at the far end of Jalan Kamunting, it is still a nice place to stay in especially for those who are on vacation *en masse*. Of late, there had been a disclosure that Jim was allegedly seen by a gardener when he came over to the premises. It was said both of them exchanged hellos. The teenager, who was in the midst of weeding a flower bed, remembered seeing Jim with a camera around his neck. While he was in the compound, he spent about ten minutes taking photographs of the place. After he had done so, he waved goodbye to the youngster. This report was not true. What actually happened was that when he came over to the habitat, he was seen by a cook named Che Fatimah binte Mohamed Yeh. She told the police she saw him at 4pm. Her testimony was published in the press three days after Jim went missing. As for the gardener, his allegation was made known 40 years later. Of the two, it is obvious the gardener was not telling the truth. To begin with, Jim did not have a camera when he came over to the enclave. The same could also be said of the Lings. The only one who had a camera was Constance. She brought it along with her when she joined Jim and the Lings for their holiday at Moonlight.

Malayan Communist Party: Refer to **Chin Peng** in Epilogue section.

Moonlight bungalow: Located at A47, Jalan Kamunting, the cottage is still a draw for the many who have had an interest in the mystery surrounding Jim's eclipse from the Cameron Highlands. The unit was first built by a British company to accommodate its staff. After the Emergency, it was sold to the Lings. Later, it became the property of an Ipoh lawyer. Over the years, the ownership of the estate has changed hands many times. Before the present owners moved in, the premises belonged to a Chinese businessman followed by a resident from Kuala Lumpur. Later it was taken over by a Caucasian who then sold it to a hotelier. In the past the house was rented out for RM750 a day. The longest residing occupant was a Japanese tourist who stayed at the place for more than a month. His food bill amounted to more than RM200 a day. Recently, there had been talk that the pre-War mansion is haunted. Unlikely. If it were so, the value of the villa would not have appreciated. Today, it is worth more than a million US dollars.

Orchard Road: The shopping district of Singapore.

Padang Besar: A border town situated in the north of Perlis, West Malaysia. The town on the Thai side of the border is also called Padang Besar. To differentiate between the two, the Malaysians prefer to call the Thai town *Pekan Siam* or Siamese Town.

Pre-War: A period before the First World War (1914 – 1918) or the Interwar period before the outbreak of the Second World War (1939 - 1945).

Raja kramat (*ra-jah kra-mud*): A Malay word meaning 'spirit king'.

Sadao: A provincial town in Southern Thailand.

Samloh (*some-law*): A Thai word meaning 'pedicab'.

Second World War: A military conflict which was fought in the last century where more than 70 million people died. The war started on September 1, 1939, when Germany invaded Poland. This was followed by the declaration of war on Germany and Japan by the countries in the British Empire and the Commonwealth of Nations. Prior to this, China and Japan were engaged in the Second Sino-Japanese War which commenced on July 7, 1937. The Second World War ended on September

9, 1945. Many countries, which were not linked to the war, were later drawn into it. This was due to the German invasion of the Soviet Union and the Japanese attacks on the European colonies in Southeast Asia. The Americans became embroiled in the war when the Japanese attacked Pearl Harbor on December 7, 1941. The war ended in 1945 in a victory for the Allies. After the war, the Soviet Union and the United States emerged as the world's superpowers. This set the stage for the Cold War which went on for the next 46 years. The Cold War ended in 1991 with the collapse of the Soviet Union.

Singapura: The old name for Singapore.

Southeast Asia Treaty Organisation (SEATO): An organization comprising eight countries which signed the Southeast Asia Collective Defense Treaty in Manila, the Philippines on September 8, 1954. The countries in the alliance were Australia, France, Great Britain, New Zealand, Pakistan, the Philippines, Thailand and the United States. The treaty was spearheaded by the United States after the French were defeated in Indochina. The US felt that a grouping was needed to put a check to the spread of communism in Southeast Asia. Over time, however, SEATO did not develop into an effective organization. It failed, in part, because countries such as India, Indonesia and Japan did not join the association. Further, its members were usually in disagreement on the extent of the communist threat in Southeast Asia. Of the eight, only Australia, New Zealand and Thailand were active participants in America's involvement in the Vietnam War (1957-1975). Pakistan withdrew from SEATO on November 7, 1973. France did likewise on June 30, 1974. Two years after the war in Vietnam came to an end, SEATO ceased to exist.

Sunlight bungalow: Located at A46, Jalan Kamunting, the unit was constructed at the same time as Moonlight. In the past, it was used by a British company to house its staff. Sunlight is about 50 meters from where Jim resided. The chateau can be rented out on a short- or long-term basis. It can easily accommodate up to 10 persons. Unlike some hotels in the area, Sunlight is compact and comfortably furnished. The rooms are spacious and exude an informal atmosphere. It is about three kilometers away from Brinchang.

Subang: A parliamentary constituency in the state of Selangor, West Malaysia. It is also the name of a small town in the state's Petaling district. The Sultan Abdul Aziz Shah Airport (the former Subang International Airport) is situated in this county. The airport was officially opened to traffic on August 30, 1965. With the opening of the Kuala Lumpur International Airport in 1998, Subang International Airport has now taken on a secondary role. It is presently a center for general aviation and turbo-prop flights.

Tapah: An administrative town in the district of Batang Padang, Perak, West Malaysia. The population of Tapah is about 80,000.

Thai Spirit altar: An outdoor structure where offerings of food and flowers are made to a selected deity. The design of the spirit house is usually similar to that of an oriental temple. But there are several factors that have to be taken into consideration before an altar could be classified as consecrated. A fine example would be the selection of an appropriate spot to position the raised structure. If space permits, it is a common practice that it be placed just outside the house. Other than that, it is normal for it be sited on top of a roof. Of utmost importance, however, is the timing the spirit takes up residence in the altar. This is customarily left to the judgment of either a Buddhist or Brahmin monk.

The Cameron Highlands: The retreat is still accessible by road via the towns of Tapah or Simpang Pulai. For non-residents of Southeast Asia it would be better to head for the resort via Kuala Lumpur. The fare for a taxi trip from the airport to the haunt is about RM250 (US$65). The other option is to travel by taxi from the airport to the Pudu Raya bus station. The fare is approximately RM70. From here there are a few bus services which ply directly to the haven. For an update of the bus schedule, please visit *http://www.cameronhighlands.com.*

The Emergency: A war for independence fought between the British and the Malayan Communist Party. The unrest began in 1948 and ended 12 years later. The *Malayan Emergency* was the colonial government's term for the conflict; the Malayan Communist Party preferred to classify it as the *Anti-British National Liberation War.*

The Japanese Occupation: A period between 1942 and 1945 when Japan controlled a vast area of the Asia-Pacific region. The countries or territories which came under its authority included Burma (Myanmar), Cambodia (Kampuchea), China, Guam, Hong Kong, Indonesia, Malaysia, Manchuria, Singapore, Thailand, Vietnam and the Philippines. On August 6, 1945, the Americans dropped the atomic bomb on Hiroshima; three days later, Nagasaki was hit. The bombing of the two cities brought the war to an end. The Japanese surrendered on August 15, 1945,

The Jim Thompson Mystery Trail: The path refers to Trail 4 which leads to the Parit Waterfall. You can start your walk from the Forestry Department or at the side of the Century Pines Resort. The route was used in the past for those who preferred to avoid walking down the main road. The distance of the sidewalk is about half a mile (0.8 km). The track got its name after an employee from the Eastern Hotel (now the Century Pines Resort) saw Jim taking the path on the day he was reported as missing. But his description of Jim was not as one would expect. As such, his evidence was not taken seriously.

The Jim Thompson website: Launched on September 7, 2009, *http://www.jimthompson.sg* is a lot different when compared to the other websites that have dwelled on the life and disappearance of Jim Thompson. The website is made up of several pages. The "quiz" page comes complete with a set of seven questions. To participate in the quiz, all you need to do is to answer the questions and click the "SUBMIT" button. You may send in as many entries as you want. Only one gold coin will be given away. The first person to get all the answers correct will be declared the winner. The answers to the quiz will be made known once an all-correct entry is received.

The Main Range: Running along the backbone of the country, the Main Range or *Banjaran Titiwangsa* is the most prominent mountain group in Peninsula Malaysia. It stretches for 300 miles (500kms) from the border of Thailand. The densely forested range gives rise to the river systems of Perak and Pahang. From Negeri Sembilan, its elevation diminishes until it touches the coastal plain of Melaka. Its western flanks are noted for its rich deposits of alluvial tin. At its center, the range extends eastward and ends at Gunung Tahan, the country's highest peak.

The Most Exalted Order of the White Elephant: A decoration given by the Thai government to individuals for the unusual services rendered to the country. It was established in 1861 by King Rama IV (1804 – 1868). Jim was given the award in 1962.

The Oriental: Located on the banks of the Chao Phraya River, the inn was the first hotel to be built in Bangkok. It was burnt down in 1865. Several years later, another hotel was constructed in its place. During the Second World War, the hotel was used by the Japanese as an officer's mess. After the war, Jim and his partners worked on the restoration of the hotel. Jim left the partnership over a plan to build a new wing. The hotel has undergone many changes since it reopened for business on June 12, 1947. In 1958, the ten-storey Garden Wing was built. It featured the city's first elevator and was home to the Le Normandie Restaurant. In 1993, the hotel opened its renowned Oriental Spa. It completed the renovation of its rooms and suites in 2003. Three years later, it celebrated its 130th anniversary. In September 2008, the hotel underwent a change in name. Today, it is known as the Mandarin Oriental, Bangkok.

The Raffles Hotel: Named after Singapore's founder Sir Stamford Raffles, the establishment is one of the few 19th century hotels left in this world. A stay at any one of its 103 suites is an experience in itself. Of late, there has been talk that one of its rooms has been distinctively named as the 'Jim Thompson Suite'. This is incorrect. The unit which has been mistakenly referred to is the 'John Thomson Suite'. John, a professional photographer, arrived in Singapore on board the P&O steamer "Emeu" in 1862. Shortly after his arrival, he set up his 'Photographic Room' at No. 3 Beach Road. He left Singapore in 1865. After spending some time in China, he returned to England in 1872. Fourteen years later, he was called upon to serve as an instructor with the Royal Geographical Society. In recognition of his role and contribution to early photography, the hotel named one of its suites after him.

The Time Tunnel: A "must visit" place if you want to get to know more about the Cameron Highlands. It is located within the Kok Lim Strawberry Farm, Jalan Sungei Burung, 39100, Brinchang. The gallery is open daily from 9am to 6pm. It is filled with *objets de art* that showcase the spirit of Malaysian life. Apart from antiques, there is an assortment of old photographs on display here – most dating back to the pre-War years.

The Time Tunnel has been around for more than three years. It has played host to more than 30,000 visitors. The admission charge is RM5 for adults and RM3 for children. There are no restrictions to photography at the museum.

The Thai Silk Company: The firm which Jim helped to establish in 1948 continues to grow to this day. It is the only silk company which has control of practically every aspect of its business, that is, from the cultivation of silk worms to the retailing of its finished products. Today, more than a hundred shareholders have a stake in the company.

The Triads: A term used to describe the many branches of Chinese secret societies based in China, Macau, Malaysia, Hong Kong, Singapore and Taiwan. Their activities include armed robbery, car theft, contact killing, racketeering, extortion, money laundering, gambling, prostitution and drug trafficking. Today, a major source of their income comes from the counterfeiting of computer software, foreign currencies, luxury wear, movie DVDs and tobacco products. The triads are Asia's equivalent of the Mafia. They are also active in cities such as New York, Los Angeles, Vancouver and the San Francisco Bay Area.

Tiger general: The supreme leader of a Chinese secret society (see **The Triads**).

Ye Olde Smokehouse: Built in 1939, the hotel has not changed much since the time Jim was reported as lost. The inn is renowned for celebrating everything British. It is still a favorite place for visitors to gather for their afternoon tea and scones.

WA